HOW TO SURVEY
YOUR CONDO ASSOCIATION

BY

DAVID F. WRENCH

authorHOUSE®

AuthorHouse™
1663 Liberty Drive, Suite 200
Bloomington, IN 47403
www.authorhouse.com
Phone: 1-800-839-8640

First published by AuthorHouse 2/17/2009

ISBN: 978-1-4389-2770-1 (sc)

Library of Congress Control Number: 2009901168

Printed in the United States of America
Bloomington, Indiana

This book is printed on acid-free paper.

Book design by Ben Zemel

This book is dedicated to all those volunteers – never paid and seldom thanked – who make our way of life possible.

Table of Contents

Introduction

Welcome to the Real World

The condo committee has chosen you to be the lead person in doing their biennial survey of membership. You may be extremely well qualified, or your main qualification may be a willingness to learn. In either case, however, one thing is true: If there is anyone else who is better qualified to do the job they are not admitting it. Qualified or not you are it.

You probably have one main liaison person on the board. It may be the chair, the secretary, or an individual member. Let's hope that it is not a subcommittee, for we would like to get this job done some time in the foreseeable future.

Suppose your contact person tells you that you will head a subcommittee to do the job, and names a couple of other members who are going to serve on it. You call them to a meeting and discuss the first things that need to be done. Although each of them agrees to undertake some specific task, they seem very reluctant to do so, as well as being resistant to accepting your leadership. You have never had this problem before - usually you are very successful at leading a group. One member's task is to draft the cover letter that will accompany the questionnaire. When you suggest a slight change in wording he sends an angry e-mail to your contact person without discussing the matter with you first. WHAT IS GOING ON?

In this case, which actually happened to me, here is what was going on: The other "members" had neither volunteered to serve on a committee nor been told that one existed. They thought they were volunteering to be among the people who took and commented on the first draft of the questionnaire. When each was asked if he or she would independently do some other task instead, each had reluctantly agreed. Little wonder they had showed no interest in hearing of the broader mission of their committee - there was no committee. Little wonder that one of them objected when the chairman criticized his work - there was no chairman.

That seems absurd. It is absurd, but it is the kind of thing that happens when one leaves academe to work in the real world.

Chapter One:
General Orientation

Are You Ready?

This is a good time to consider your qualifications for doing the job. The example above was given to explain why it is that a sense of humor is probably the most important requirement. It is very hard to know when you have managed to establish something so that you can count on it. Dates that are agreed to are arbitrarily changed because of something that had not been thought of. The firm approval that you have for your procedures suddenly becomes less firm when they are criticized by someone at a higher level – or off on a parallel one. The person you thought had the authority to authorize your study is overruled by someone else who turns out to have the real authority, even if not officially. There is a reason why the French military thought that a sense of humor was the first requirement of a staff officer.

The next requirement is stubbornness. You will have to stick to your guns, and go back to convince the fourth person, just as you did the first three – and sometimes the same one more than once. Only change if you encounter someone with great expertise in the area. If you do, take advantage of it, up to and including letting him or her do the job. Otherwise you are right and he is wrong. Don't forget it.

It goes without saying that you should not be afraid of either math or computers. Again it is not specific knowledge that is required, but a determination that you can and will learn the things that you do not yet know. When I took statistics in graduate school I frequently found that I could not solve a particular problem no matter how long I spent on it. If I came back the next day it often became immediately clear. This would not happen without the hard work the day before, but it did happen. So do not be discouraged if there is some part of what you are doing that you just do not seem to get. Work at it, get away from it, work at it again, and be prepared for that glorious moment what you suddenly see that it is really very simple.

This brings us to the final characteristic that you need in order to be able to do the study. You need to be very persuasive.

The Nature of the Task

At first glance it would seem that surveying a group such as the membership of your association should be a snap. You write a few questions, tabulate the answers, and write up the results. What could be easier?

You can see that it is not that easy if you think about some of the bad questionnaires that you have answered – or refused to answer -- in the past. Some had questions with multiple-choice answers that failed to include the answers you wanted to give. Others had a group of questions about a topic that did not include ones about those aspects of the topic that you considered most important.

In many cases the questionnaire and the way it was administered may have failed to establish the trust that would make you willing to answer it. It may have been an obvious sales pitch disguised as an attitude survey. Or the wording of the questions may have revealed the point of view of the questioner to such an extent that you could see that the survey was biased.

The failings of those questionnaires should tell you two things. One is that writing a questionnaire is not so easy that any fool can do it. Apparently a number of fools already have. The other is that you already know a great deal about what to do if you just think about what you do know.

Besides those failings that you can see by reading the questionnaire, there are many others that you cannot see. These include such things as inadequate sampling and inaccurate coding. The most important of them, however, is giving meaning to things that are meaningless. Telling which differences are meaningful and which aren't is the realm of statistics, and we will have to explore that realm to some extent. Be of good cheer, however, for we will not have to go into that field at any great depth.

Box #1-1 lists the steps involved in a typical survey. There may be fewer if you are the Chair of the Board and have its complete trust. There may be even more if you have difficult people to work with. In any case you should plan on the process taking at least two months, and probably three.

BOX I-1: TO-DO LIST
Why the study won't be done
in a week or two.

1. Informally discuss project with Board.
2. With help of board recruit team members.
3. Get board to authorize your proceeding.
4. Solicit possible items from committees, groups.
5. Meet with team members to discuss plans.
6. Make tentative decision as to what is practical.
7. Make first draft of questions and plan analysis.
8. Solicit heterogeneous volunteers for pretest.
9. Finalize and reproduce pretest questionnaire.
10. Give pretest, thanking participants.
11. Consider results, content analyzing open-ended questions.
12. Get board's authorization to continue.
13. Go over questionnaire & coding instructions.
14. Do cover letter to accompany questionnaire.
15. Get board to approve of their cover letter. Expect them to want a lawyer to approve.
16. Obtain & correct lists of owners and residents.
17. Get the agreement of your work group for the questionnaires/ procedures/coding plans.
18. Get questionnaires printed & distributed.
19. Check in questionnaires as returned.
20. Start coding data, checking accuracy.
21. Improve procedures to lower error rate.
22. Finish data coding and do analysis.
23. Write report (or reports.)
24. Distribute them.

Some General Principles

We will be discussing a lot of specifics in the course
of this book, but first let us look at some general
principles that you should follow whatever the
specifics.

- The first principle is that you should be very
  clear about the purpose of the study and the
  population that you are sampling.

- The second is one we have already hinted at: Do
  not give respondents any clue that you might
  agree with or prefer one answer rather than
  another.

- The third is that you should promise anonymity
  and live up to that promise.

- The fourth is that context is central to
  communication. You must provide the appropriate
  context in communicating to your respondents
  and consider context in interpreting their
  answers. Let us look at these in more depth.

Who. When you start out it may seem obvious that
the population you are studying is made up of the
members of the condo association. Actually, however,
it depends of what questions you are asking. If you
want to know the level of some service - such as
window washing, for example - that the members
want to contract for, then the owners are the relevant
group. But if you want to know about the experience
of living in the condominium, then you want to get
the impressions of everyone living there - renters as
well as owners. Think of it this way: If the association
members owned the building but none of them lived

7

there, wouldn't they still want to survey their tenants to find out what was working and what wasn't working as the building was currently being managed? You may well want to have two parts to your survey - one to be answered by all owners and one by all residents.

One important thing to keep in mind - and to tell the people you are surveying - is that the survey is not a vote of the condo association. It is advisory to the board, who will want to consider the information it provides but will use their own judgment how to use - or not use - that information in the decisions they make.

There are many situations where the board will have good reason for not going along with a preference of the membership. Consider, for example, a condo association whose members thought that the board should be very tolerant of owners being late with their condo fees, with nothing being done until the owner was at least four months in arrears. It is easy to see why the board would not go along with such a policy.

Just deciding whether you are surveying owners, or residents, or both, does not completely answer the question of what population you are sampling. There are going to be multiple owners of some units, and multiple renters living in a unit, and association members who own multiple units. How are you going to deal with those situations?

The rules that my condo association followed in their survey were "One unit, one questionnaire" and "More than one unit, still one questionnaire." The first of these is in accord with the rules for actual votes by the association; the second is not. Though nobody seemed to notice when this was violated at a recent annual meeting, the rules for votes specify that owners of multiple units get as many votes as they have units. It was not of great importance at that meeting for there are relatively few rentals in the building and the votes were close to unanimous. Still the ownership situation - and the precedents on voting – may differ greatly in different associations. In deciding what rule to follow you should be sensitive to the sentiment in the organization. If you have any choice, however, go with the procedure that the survey here followed. It is the easiest one to implement.

If your Association is very large you may want to survey only a sample. Here it is important to draw it so that it is representative. Doing a phone interview, for example, will catch different groups of people at different times of the day. Letting people self-select is most dangerous. (See Box I-2)

BOX I-2
Sampling: The Literary Digest poll

Often we cannot question all of the people whose opinions are of interest to us. Where this is the case it is very important that the ones we do question are representative of the entire group. Perhaps the first dramatic example of this was given in the Presidential election of 1936. The Literary Digest mailed questionnaires to a very large sample of individuals drawn from lists of telephone subscribers and automobile owners. They predicted that Alfred Landon would beat Franklin D. Roosevelt by a substantial margin. A neophyte in the area, George Gallup, questioned a much smaller scientifically drawn sample and did not depend on voluntary return of questionnaires. His prediction of a victory by FDR proved correct. The Literary Digest had made two mistakes. In 1936 many people did not have either a telephone or an automobile. This error was compounded by reliance on voluntary return of the questionnaires. People dissatisfied with FDR were more likely to respond,

Even if you have a good sample to begin with your results may be thrown off if people of one persuasion are more inclined to respond than those of another. Comparing individuals who respond to a first request with those who have to be reminded one or more times can help you estimate the size of this potential error. Especially important is the question of whether the ones who are reluctant to answer feel more or less strongly about the issues than the ones who are eager to do so. If they feel less strongly they may just be people who do not take much interest in condo affairs. If they are the ones who feel strongly, the board has a problem on its hands. It means that potentially active people do not have enough trust to tell you what they are thinking.

Why. Wanting to know the answer is not the only reason for asking a question. We have already noted that it might be done to aid a sales campaign. Some other reasons are

To make the association members feel that something is being done about an issue they are worked up about.

To start them thinking about possibilities that you soon will propose.

To ask the questions in a biased way that will make it appear that there is support for some course of action that you have already decided on or

To plant erroneous information in the minds of the respondents in the guise of asking questions.

This guide assumes that you really do want to find out the truth of what the membership believes and prefers - not, for example, what would be most comforting to you. It will not bother me very much as author, if you are also trying to calm an upset membership, or to raise ideas that they might think about in the future. If you are asking slanted questions in order to get biased results, try to rethink that objective. If push polling is what you have in mind, go wash your mouth out with soap. (See Box I-3.)

BOX I-3
THE MISUSE OF AN ATTITUDE SURVEY: PUSH POLLING

One of the dirtiest political strategies to arise in recent years is based on a finding of social psychology called the "sleeper effect." What that states is that information that you get from a source that you distrust becomes more persuasive as time passes. It is as if you remembered the information but forgot that you had acquired it from a source in which you had no faith.

The way it works is that respondents are asked hypothetical questions containing scurrilous information about some one or thing. There is no claim that the information is true, it is only part of a question about how the respondent would feel if it were true. However, the respondent remembers the information and comes to believe it as the source is forgotten:

"Would you favor Lincoln running again if you knew that his wife was a confederate spy?"

"Would you support Jefferson Davis if you found out that he was making a fortune on kickbacks from military suppliers?"

In time the people who were supposedly being polled come to believe that there is doubt about the loyalty of Mrs. Lincoln or the integrity of President Davis.

Being and Appearing Impartial. Most people have little idea how much they telegraph their opinions. Again your own experience probably provides an illustration, for when you were in school you probably had teachers who gave multiple-choice tests. I will assume that usually you had the material cold, but ask you to remember those rare instances when you didn't have a clue. Now, about what proportion of the questions could you guess when that was the case? A third? Half? More?

If you are reasonably bright the odds are that you could guess about a half. If you were brighter than the teacher, probably more. There are innumerable ways

12

in which most teachers hint at the correct answer without realizing it.

Some have a position preference, and make answers in that position right more than their share of the time. Others introduce a different type of answer only when it is right, or have two false answers mean the same thing so that they must both be wrong, etc., etc.

There are fewer ways to telegraph you own views in an attitude survey than there are on a multiple choice test, but there are still enough so that few people can avoid giving clues as to their own attitudes when writing one. It is extremely difficult to recognize judgmental language when we use it. Advocates of different positions habitually use different terms for the same thing, so that by using one word or the other you are tipping your hand. In surveying your membership you are probably going to focus very much on budgetary items. You must avoid characterizing things as "potential savings" or "service cuts." You can describe the present level of service and give its cost. You can list other possible levels of that same service - (more of this later) - but you absolutely must avoid judgmental terms you would use in everyday speech without a second thought.

In a way it is fortunate that you probably do not have the resources to interview subjects individually, for it is even more difficult to conceal you feelings when you interact face-to-face. Your emotional reactions are so obvious that even a horse can read them, as was shown by the case of Clever Hans. Hans was a horse who seemed able to do arithmetic. You would ask him, "How much is three and two?" and he would tap his hoof five times. What made this impressive was that his trainer did not have to be present for Hans to perform. Anyone could ask him the questions.

Psychologist Oskar Pfungst discovered what was going on. The person who asked the question leaned forward while the horse tapped his hoof. When the horse reached the correct answer the questioner relaxed. Fungst demonstrated that Hans would go on tapping as long as the questioner leaned forward and stop when the questioner leaned back. Hans' trainer, no more aware of the nonverbal clues he was giving than anyone else is, really thought that he had taught Hans to do arithmetic.

Since we seldom see our own biases, you and the other members of your team need to read each other's contributions. That is especially helpful if the person doing the reading has very different views from the one writing the material. Unfortunately, that is seldom the case. Doing a pretest of your draft instrument can help, but it is better to catch these things before you reach that stage.

Anonymity. Most administrators find the idea of having the survey anonymous foreign to them. They are equally upset by the thought that someday the questionnaires will be destroyed. They generally believe that everything should be recorded and that all the records should be kept as long as human civilization exists. Surely the comments that people make would be more meaningful if you knew who made them! Besides, you could learn so many useful things. Maybe you could catch individuals who were illegally renting their condos. After all doesn't "anonymous" really just mean that only the few people administering the questionnaire will know whose is whose?

No, "anonymous" means that **nobody** knows whose questionnaire is whose. It is impossible to exaggerate how important this is. To a professional working in this area, violating a promise of confidentiality is as inconceivable as it would be for a priest to violate the sanctity of the confessional. Unless the confidentiality is absolute people will not feel free to tell the whole truth. Furthermore, the person who does violate it has destroyed the trust on which his or her professional self is based. This is the kind of issue that tenured professors resign over.

One of the most famous lines in the English language was spoken by a little furry animal in a comic strip. I refer of course to Pogo's statement that "We have met the enemy and they is us." Maintaining the confidentiality of questionnaires is one of the places where this great truth applies. You may have others, such as the Chair of the Board, demand that you use the questionnaire to surreptitiously spy on the members, but you are far more likely to have to fight temptation in yourself. Do so. This is one non-negotiable area.

To avoid temptation what you need to do is to use a procedure where you could not cheat if you wanted to. It is also important that the procedure should be one where the respondents can see that to be the case. If it weren't for that latter consideration it would suffice to have all identification on a top sheet to the questionnaire that would be torn off as soon as you had recorded that so-and-so had turned in his or hers. That procedure, however, might not convince respondents that nobody was looking at their answers before the sheet was torn off.

In the recent survey of my condo we used a system often used for mail-in ballots, as it is in Oregon. The questionnaire is returned in an outer envelope that has all the identification that is wanted - in the case of votes, even a signature to guarantee the authenticity of the contents. When the response is received one person checks off that a ballot or questionnaire has been received from that person. He removes the inner secrecy envelope from the outer one and hands it to another person who puts a code number on it. That will be its only identification from that point on. The first person destroys the outer envelope and the second person never sees it. The first person does not see what code number the other has put on it. At no point is the identity of the respondent linked to the questionnaire's identity number.

At this point the administrator is likely to object, "But shouldn't you keep the information just in case..." Just in case what? Just in case you want to cheat? There is no legitimate reason for having the information identifying whose questionnaire is whose. It should not exist.

Years ago, when I was one of a group of graduate teaching assistants, the department head would periodically come into our office and ask how things were going. No matter how impossible the work, none of us ever complained. Instead we said that things were going just fine. "That's what I want to hear," was often her reply. The manner in which she asked the question made clear that a positive reply was the only acceptable one. In general it is very difficult - and often unwise - for anyone who is under someone else's authority to tell the truth to that someone else. That is one of the obstacles to a good relationship between parent and child, and it is why questionnaires must be anonymous if you want the answers to be a sound guide for policy.

Although the matter of anonymity is the main one where living up to your word may be an issue, it is not the only one. It is very helpful to get free responses from members of your sample as well as endorsement of fixed alternatives. One individual may notice something that everyone else has overlooked, such as a fire door that is habitually left open or a small water leak in an inconspicuous place. Give opportunities to comment sparingly, however. By getting unstructured responses you are implicitly promising that they will be read and considered. Be sure that you are able to live up to that promise by not getting any more than you and your colleagues will be able to read.

Context. Probably there is more deception, especially unintentional deception, brought about by providing inadequate context than comes about in any other way. Historian Rodolfo Acuña gives a simple example. Look up "Louisiana Purchase" in an encyclopedia. You will probably read that we acquired the Louisiana Purchase on April 11, 1803, agreeing to pay France $15 million for it. The discussion may go on the point out that with the settling of past debts plus interest the ultimate cost was over $23 million. You may even be surprised, as I was, to find that it stretched so far north that it included parts of present day Saskatchewan.

So, what is wrong with that information? Nothing as far as it goes. It is true, but it is not the whole truth. Taken by itself it implies that France had effective sovereignty over the area. It does not mention that we agreed to pay over three times that amount to Indian tribes living in the area, and that the treaties with them took over ten years more to negotiate. If we know that additional information we get a more accurate picture of the state of affairs during the period of the acquisition. We knew that France did not have effective sovereignty.

Similarly, leaving out a small part of a quotation may greatly alter its meaning. The frequently quoted phrase "My country right or wrong" gives quite a different flavor from the more complete quotation, "My country, may she ever be right, but right or wrong, my country."

The recent study of my own condo illustrates how the matter of context can enter into attitude measurement. The range of alternatives with which they are presented influences the answers that people give. Because that survey was being administered at a time when cost cutting was in the air, the inclination was to ask "Where, and by how much, should we cut?" Asking in that way, however, would be reminiscent of a W.C. Fields film in which the townspeople are about to hang him. He objects that he should be given a trial, and one of them responds, "Right. First we'll try you and then we'll hang you."

For the attitude survey to come up with accurate information on people's preferences it was essential that the questions not be written with the presumption that costs and services should be cut. The instrument that was used gave respondents the chance to choose enhanced as well as reduced service. Not giving that alternative would be like asking "How much money are you willing to give to the Republican Presidential candidate?" and then reporting some average amount as reflecting the respondents' political feelings without considering how much they would give to other candidates.

Besides you providing the respondents with context for them to use in answering the questions, they can provide you with context to help you interpret their answers. The most important thing they can tell you is how strongly they feel about the different issues.

Have you ever thought about how often a Congressman will adopt a position on an issue that is at odds with the position held by most of his or her constituents? Consider gun control. A majority of voters favor stricter regulation in that area, but it just doesn't happen. As everyone knows, that is because the National Rifle Association is so influential. Most voters have opinions on the subject, but NRA members are willing to donate money, lobby tirelessly, hire television time, and do anything they can to influence the outcome. Politicians who go against them do so at great risk of not being re-elected. You cannot understand what is happening without knowing how strongly various people feel about the issue. The same thing is true in the attitude survey you will be doing. You don't just have to measure people's attitudes. On important items you must also measure how strongly they feel about the matter, if you want to understand what is going on.

Summary

In a variety of different ways this chapter has been discussing the first great requirement for an adequate study of attitudes -- obtaining, deserving, and keeping the trust of your subjects. That trust is developed by the respondents being able to see that you are making a serious effort to understand their points of view. The questionnaire must cover the topics that they consider relevant to that universe of discourse, and the multiple choice answers – if you use fixed response items – should ideally include every answer that one of them might want to give. (Since that is impossible, one alternative is to give multiple-choice answers, plus a blank to write in one's own answer if none of the listed ones suffices.)

Trust is fragile, and can be undermined by any wording that appears biased or equally by your failure to live up to your commitments. Central to its development is your not only guaranteeing anonymity, but using procedures that make clear that you could not violate that anonymity even if you wanted to. The study does not begin with the questionnaire, but with your developing a relationship of mutual trust with the respondents.

A SAMPLE COVER LETTER

FROM: The XXX Board of Directors   March X ,2008

SUBJECT: Survey of Expectations and Satisfaction

TO: Member, XXX Condominium Owners Association
                  Resident, XXX Condominiums

The XXX Condominium Owners Association Board of Directors is closely examining the cost of utilities, services, maintenance, management and administrative support for the XXX. The objective of this comprehensive examination is the reduction of costs while also maintaining expected facilities, services and quality-of-life. The recent increase in unit monthly assessments for 2008 has sharpened our efforts. This increase was primarily due to previous underestimates for utilities (40%), facilities maintenance (16%) and the fair reallocation of facilities maintenance costs between the owners of residential and commercial units. A portion of your monthly assessment must, by

YYY state statutes, be set aside in a reserve account for those common elements which require maintenance and eventual repair or replacement. Currently, approximately 12% of your monthly assessment is reserved for this important purpose.

To assist the Board of Directors in this endeavor, we request that you complete the attached survey. The budgetary questions are only for unit owners, covering the main discretionary services that account for approximately 30% of the 2008 budget. We are also seeking suggestions for achieving efficiencies and economies in the remaining 70% of the budget. The remaining part of the survey is for all residents to provide us with their satisfaction with facilities, amenities and services, and their opinions on policies.

This is not a formal vote of the Association. The Board of Directors is not bound to comply with the results. However, the results of the survey will be very important and help the Board of Directors determine the quality and level of services in the future. Survey choices include both reduced and enhanced service options. Service options show the associated annual budget and a per square foot cost to enable you to estimate your cost for that option using the floor space of your unit (unit area plus area of patio; see Exhibit C-3 of the Declaration of Condominium Ownership for XXX Condominiums).

This is an anonymous survey. Its administration is patterned after the vote-by-mail system used in Oregon elections. Please complete the attached survey, <u>seal it in the privacy envelope provided, insert the privacy envelope into the provided return envelope, complete the name, signature and unit number sections on the return envelope</u>. Return it to the Concierge. For nonresident owners, please try to mail it back in the provided addressed, stamped return envelope by April X, 2008. We must ensure that all surveys are valid and that there are no duplications. Consequently, we will need names, signatures and unit numbers on return envelopes. <u>A returned survey without this validation information on the return envelope will not be used</u>. After we validate the return envelope, the privacy envelope will be removed and the return envelope destroyed.

Sincerely,

Board of Directors, XXX Condominium Owners Association

Enclosed: Survey of Expectations and Satisfaction, Privacy Envelope & Return Envelope

Chapter Two:
Becoming an Expert

Self Presentation

As everyone knows, an expert is someone from out of town. That is only the half of it, however. An expert is someone from out of town *who is paid.* In proposing to do an attitude survey for the condo association you have the two great disadvantages that you are neither. Even if you have credentials recognized elsewhere, and especially if you don't, you are going to have to convince the board that you are the person for the job. That will be the case even if there are no other real alternatives. If you want them to really believe in you, and trust that you will make the right decisions even without them constantly monitoring you, you will have to convince them that you are not "just Al" – (or Phil or Maureen or whoever.)

Social psychology gives some hints on how to do this. One of the findings is that people do want to give you a break and see you as you see yourself. To some extent you can get accepted as a leader just by acting as if you thought you were the leader. One simple act has important implications – where you sit at the table. You should arrive early enough so that one end of it is free and sit there. Research has shown that you are more likely to be seen as a leader if you do so. If it is not possible or appropriate for you to sit at the end, move right into the middle of the group. Do not take a peripheral position for that communicates lack of involvement.

Similarly you should exude quiet confidence. There is a fine line between claiming competence and appearing boastful. W.S. Gilbert was only partly right when he wrote that, "If you want in this world to advance...you must stir it and stump it and blow your own trumpet, or trust me you haven't a chance." True up to a point, but don't overdo it.

Another caution: You must be protective of the self-conceptions of others if you want them to be protective of yours. Do not claim more competence than the other person has in an area *that is central to his or her self-conception.* If she is a statistician, say that you only know a little about the area and look forward to getting help from her on statistical matters.

Negotiation

Over the last few decades social theory has very much changed in how it sees culture. We used to see societies as socializing each generation in its turn in a cultural pattern which, in the absence of technological innovation, might go on until the end of time.
There was some basis for this view, as has been shown in the recent resurgence of ethnic identities. Kurds dream of restoring greater Kurdistan, and groups that I ignorantly thought of as existing only in Biblical times, such as Hittites, are alive and well as ethnic groups in the United States today.

What that view left out is that cultures may show continuity, but it is not just by the enculturation of the succeeding generations. Cultures are dynamic, and are recreated anew all the time. When you interact with another person you are not mechanically acting out a role that you were socialized in. You are negotiating your role with the other person. Your shared culture has taught each of you the moves, but the game is constantly played anew.

Maybe one way of illustrating this is with an example from one of Tony Hillerman's Navaho mysteries. A nonbeliever ridicules a ceremony because this supposedly ancient form uses a modern physical artifact that could not have existed until long after the supposed origin of the ceremony. He is told that the particular artifact that plays the role is totally unimportant – the niche exists and continues whatever fills it. Thus what it means to be a Hittite, or a Jew, or an Episcopalian, or a Mayan is constantly reinvented, filling old forms with new clay – but also modifying the forms.

According to this view, when you appear before the board you are not asking to be allowed to step into a defined social niche with rights and obligations that are mutually understood and agreed-on. Instead you are inventing what it means to be the person who is doing their survey. It is not enough for you to get the job. You need to get it on your terms.

There are worse things than not getting the job. One of them is getting the job with you being defined as their subordinate, to use whatever technical skill you have to carry out their directives. You need to make clear that you will not accept the job on those terms. You are the expert. They can tell you their goals. How you achieve those goals is up to you. In the best of circumstances your threat to pull out if you cannot do the job on your terms remains implicit. If things go less well it may need to be explicit. You should not make it unless you are willing to carry it out. If you lose the job, so be it. It is better than being cast as a peon.

The trouble is that the members of the board see themselves as the head Honchos, so you are in that situation where defending your self-conception attacks theirs. In the case of my study of my condo the challenge came when one board member indicated that I should include a lot of open-ended questions in the survey. I said that I hoped that he had someone to read the responses, as I certainly wasn't going to. The discussion passed on to other topics. Eventually I got provisional acceptance from the person who had challenged me when I showed him, (a professional computer programmer) – that I did know something about methodology.

Finally, and here's the rub, you are more likely to be accepted as a leader if you really do know what you are talking about. This is the point where we are going to start making that happen. The rest of this chapter and parts of succeeding ones are a crash course in methodology.

Being Prepared

What are we doing talking about how to interpret data here at the beginning? Isn't that what you do near the end?

There are two reasons for talking about it here. The first, as you have seen, is that there are a few things that you should know in order to appear qualified when you interact with the board. The other is that you must plan how you are going to analyze your data before you collect any or you may find that the data you have collected are impossible to analyze. In this section we will focus on the former, leaving more specific questions of questionnaire design and coding until a bit later.

To appear *au courant* with methodology there are a few concepts that you should be familiar with:
- What it means for results to be *significant*.
- What *nominal, ordinal, interval* and *ratio* measurement are.
- What a *normal distribution* is.
- What *parametric* and *nonparametric* statistics are.
- What *correlation* is.

There are also some practical techniques that you will eventually have to master:
- How to work with spreadsheets.
- How to do a chi-square test.
- How to make a multi-item index.
- How to develop a coding sheet

Now that may seem like a lot to learn. Actually it isn't very much, if you want to appear to be an expert on methodology. Most of the information can be presented in a few short self-contained boxes. However, you should learn it very well. Now let us look at the concepts, leaving the calculations until later.

If you enjoy working with numbers you might as well skip the first box, for its contents were not written for you.

BOX II-1
FEAR OF NUMBERS

I wonder if you are one of those lucky people who got good math instruction in school? If not, you may have received training in how not to be a mathematician. Were you taught that a problem has only one right answer? That there is only one way to do it? Criticized for thinking about things differently?

Neither of those first two dogmatic assertions is correct, and if you were taught either of them you would do well to forget it. The criticism was outrageous, for thinking differently is what the field is all about. Let's consider whether a problem has only one right answer. Do you remember what a square root is? You probably do: The square root of X is the number that multiplied by itself gives you X. Now, keeping that definition firmly in mind, what is the square root of 16?

Did I hear you say "four?" If so you are right. Four multiplied by it does give you 16. That is not the only right answer, however. Minus four multiplied by itself also gives 16. Even this simple problem has more than one right answer.

Is there more than one way to solve a problem? A mathematician may spend years trying different approaches to solving one of the unsolved problems of mathematics. Or he may come up with a new way of solving one that has already been solved. Even that would be publishable. There may be many different ways of solving a complex problem, all of them right.

There are even multiple ways of solving a simple one. Here is hard one to solve in your head: How much is 3 times 27? Even in your head you can do it the way you would do it with pencil and paper: three times seven is twenty-one. Remember the one and carry the two, etc.

Here's another way: Three times twenty-seven is the same as three times twenty plus three times seven. That is what three times twenty-seven means, isn't it? Well, 3x20=60 and 3X7=21. So three times 27 is 60+21, or 81.

If you are not used to playing with numbers that second way probably did not immediately occur to you. If you ever start to enjoy them, though, you will soon see ways like that all the time. Rather than cheating, as your teacher may have called it, that is thinking like a mathematician. Rather than a minefield of wrong answers, mathematics is a playground of possibilities.

You don't have to change a lifetime of thinking to read on, however, so relax and enjoy learning a little bit about measurement. There won't even be a quiz at the end of the week.

Statistical Significance. One of the most common errors in interpreting the results of a questionnaire study is drawing conclusions from differences that are more apparent than real. Most people, if you show them numbers, attribute meaning to the differences between them. If the janitorial service gets an average rating of 3.2 on some scale, and the window washing service only gets 3.0, they conclude that people are more satisfied with the janitors than with the window washers. That may not be the case however. The questionnaire was probably not answered by everyone in the association. If a different group of people had been included in the sample would the difference have come out in the same way? In other words, was the difference real or could it have been a matter of chance – the chance, in this case, being who answered the question and who didn't. You will use statistical tests to answer that question about your results.

A *significant* result is one that is unlikely to have occurred by chance. This has nothing to do with how important it is in real life – that is a different question. Suppose that you have been accused of cheating at cards in the wild west of the past. If convicted you will be hung. The townspeople vote and by a single vote you are acquitted. You couldn't care less that if old Joe hadn't been too hung over to come to the meeting you would have been convicted. The results may not be statistically significant, but to you they are just as important as if they were.

In interpreting the results of our study of the condo association we do care about statistical significance. The board should not base its decisions on differences that might well have come out the other way.

Let us look at an early example related to statistical significance.

BOX II-2
Sampling

Psychologists are always trying to get research subjects. Sometimes the subjects are paid. Sometimes they are required to participate in experiments as part of an introductory psychology course. As far as I know Sir Francis Galton was the first person to ask his subjects to pay for the privilege. He set up a laboratory and took every measurement he could think of on his subjects. For telling them the results he charged a small fee. His goal was to find out how a number of human traits are distributed. If a person is 1" taller than the average, how common is that? Galton, one of the pioneers of statistics, was trying to establish a databank that would enable him to judge the probability of any given deviation – such as that of a person's stature being that inch above the mean. His work contributed to statistics based on the normal curve, to which we shall return later.

Although one of the first to ask about human populations, Galton was far from the first to ask about the probability of different things happening. The first work in that area was done by other pioneers – professional gamblers calculating the probabilities of different rolls of the dice.

Just as Sir Francis did, you are going to be drawing samples and reaching conclusions. In doing this you will need the help of an expert statistician. Did you know that just such an expert is probably lurking in your computer right now? It is if you have Excel or some comparable spreadsheet program. So even if you do not have a human methodologist helping you, you have an inanimate one ready at hand. Whether your consultant is human or electronic, however, you need to know a certain amount to be able to communicate with him, her, or it. That is what reading this publication should give you.

Different significance levels. As everyone knows if they think about it a bit, improbable events do occur, they just don't occur very often. If we are going to conclude that results are *significant* if they would occur only one time in 20, (5 times in 100, or the .05 significance level), there is still the possibility that we will conclude that some finding is real when it isn't. That is also true if we set a more stringent level **- *very significant*,** (.01 or 1 time in 100) – or **extremely significant** (.001 or 1 time in 1,000.) Theoretically science does not know total certainty. Still, decisions must be made, so we are going to base them on those results that seem most likely to be true.

Levels of measurement. If basing important decisions on insignificant differences is the most common methodological error in survey research, the misuse of numbers must be a close runner-up. Numbers have different meanings depending on how they are obtained. Let us look at four of those meanings, starting with the most informative.

Suppose that you are going to tile a floor. If you started at a corner and progressed across the room, then you might well end up with rows of partial tiles along two walls, contrasting with the rows of full tiles along the walls you started with. To avoid this problem you decide to start in the center to make the wall treatments comparable

You measure the length of the room, divide by two, and draw a line. You do the same with the width. Where the two lines cross is the center and you start there. With the aid of your tape you are using *ratio* measurement. Not only are the inch marks equally spaced on your tape, (the requirement for "interval" measurement) but you also have a meaningful zero point to start measuring from – the first wall. Because of that it is meaningful to talk about the ratios of numbers to each other. You can say that where you start tiling is half of the way from one wall to the other.

Interval level measurement is what you are using if the numbers are equally far apart but you do not have a meaningful zero point. As we measure them both time and temperature are interval measurement. Units of time such as weeks are equally long, but we have no known zero point for the beginning of time. Similarly, whether we use Fahrenheit or the Centigrade, zero on the scale does not correspond to no temperature.

With an interval scale you cannot meaningfully speak of the ratio of one number to another. I cannot say that it is twice as hot at 80 degrees as it is at 40 degrees. I could make a statement like that if I were using the Absolute scale, for on that scale zero is the point at which all molecular motion stops – it is a real zero point. Similarly I cannot say that 1800 represents twice as much time as 900, for calendars use an arbitrary zero point. I could meaningfully say that some date was twice as long ago as some other date, for the present time is a meaningful point to use as a zero.

Interval and ratio scales are the ones that we normally use in everyday life. People often mistakenly use statistics designed for interval or ratio scales on numbers representing a lower level of measurement, especially ordinal measurement. (Those lower levels are illustrated in Boxes II-3 and II-4.)The power of modern computer programs makes that easy. Its been said of the computer that the problem isn't that if you ask it a stupid question it will give you a stupid answer. The problem is its doing so with a straight face.

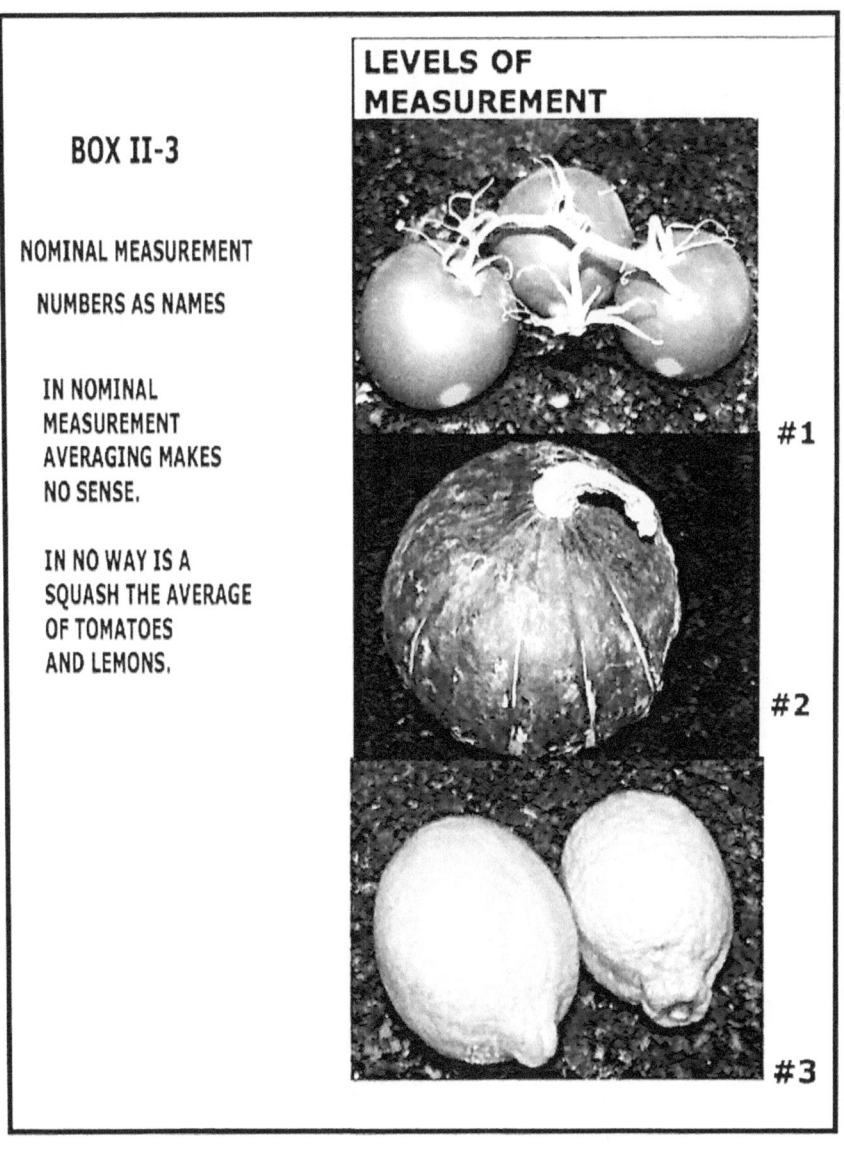

LEVELS OF MEASUREMENT

BOX II-3

NOMINAL MEASUREMENT

NUMBERS AS NAMES

IN NOMINAL MEASUREMENT AVERAGING MAKES NO SENSE.

IN NO WAY IS A SQUASH THE AVERAGE OF TOMATOES AND LEMONS.

#1

#2

#3

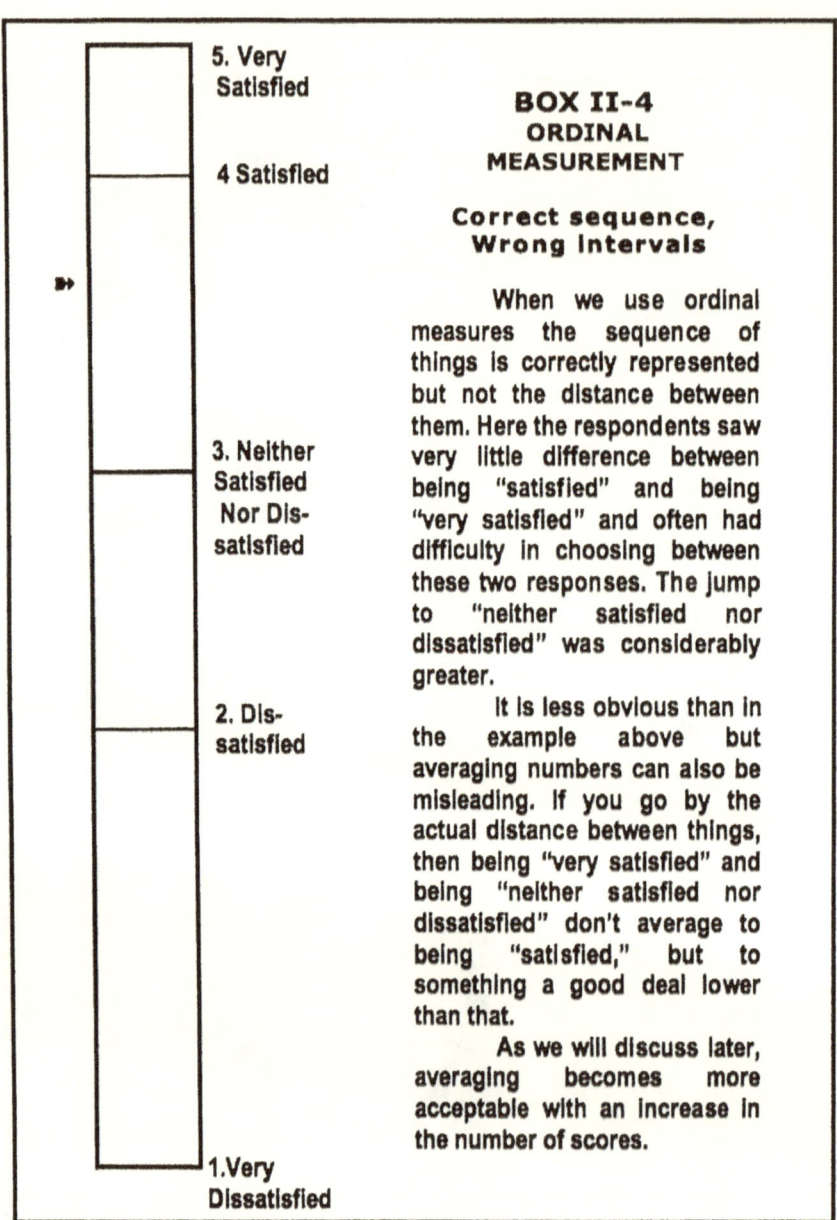

5. Very Satisfied

4 Satisfied

3. Neither Satisfied Nor Dis- satisfied

2. Dis- satisfied

1.Very Dissatisfied

BOX II-4
ORDINAL MEASUREMENT

Correct sequence, Wrong intervals

When we use ordinal measures the sequence of things is correctly represented but not the distance between them. Here the respondents saw very little difference between being "satisfied" and being "very satisfied" and often had difficulty in choosing between these two responses. The jump to "neither satisfied nor dissatisfied" was considerably greater.

It is less obvious than in the example above but averaging numbers can also be misleading. If you go by the actual distance between things, then being "very satisfied" and being "neither satisfied nor dissatisfied" don't average to being "satisfied," but to something a good deal lower than that.

As we will discuss later, averaging becomes more acceptable with an increase in the number of scores.

34

The Normal Distribution

You have probably heard of the normal distribution, or "bell-shaped curve." Why is it important? Where does it come from, and why is it "normal?"

The normal curve is important because many statistical tests are based on it. The circumstances under which you can or cannot use them will be an important theme of this chapter.

The normal curve is what you get when some score or number is influenced by many independent factors each having about the same effect. The weight distribution of individual sheep slaughtered in Australia last year, the width of tree rings over the last century, the number of ticks on a given plot each week over five years – each of those is the outcome of many factors with none having an over-riding effect and probably is normally distributed. It is because it is so pervasive that the distribution is called normal.

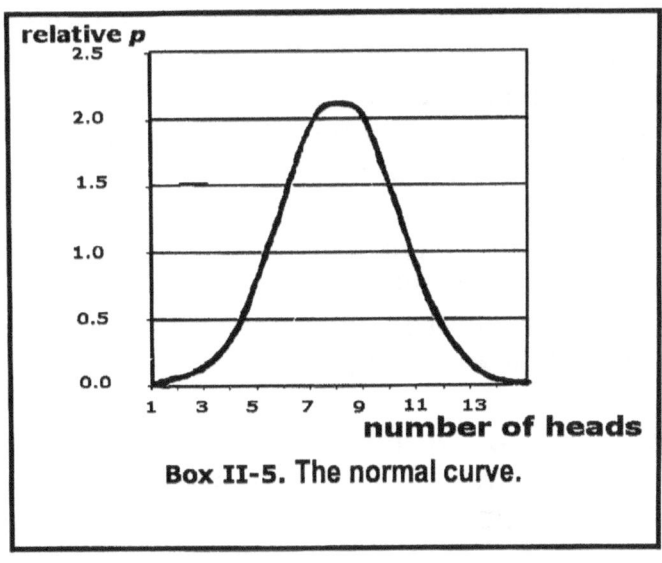

Box II-5. The normal curve.

Here is an approximation of the normal distribution, this one based on how many heads you get, on average, when you flip a coin 15 times. Each coin flip is independent of the others. The probability of getting 0 heads or 15 is so small that they do not show on the graph, while the chance of getting something near 7 or 8 is substantial.

Box 2-4 illustrates ordinal measurement, the kind that you have if you measure something with a single item. As is pointed out in Box 2-4, the different alternative answers that you present to the respondent are probably not equally spaced along the continuum of acceptance of the item. For items such as these you want to use statistics that make no assumption about the kind of measurement you have or the distribution of the scores that people are assigned. Such statistics are called **nonparametric.** The one that you will make the most use of is **chi-square.** In chapters to come you will be shown how to calculate and use it.

Now here is why this is important: Because normal distributions are so common, many statistics were developed that can be used only if the variable you are looking at is normally distributed. **Many, probably most, of the ones you will be dealing with in your study are not.** That is why one of the most common methodological errors in semi-formal research studies such as the one you are doing is using those statistics when the results will be erroneous and misleading. These include the most common measure of whether two things are related to each other, the Pearson product-moment **correlation coefficient.**

Although each of your individual items represents ordinal measurement, there are some circumstances when you can assume that you have interval level measurement. You achieve this by putting together a number of items to make an **index** that gives more accurate measurement than a single item. If the scores on the index meet certain assumptions then you can use **parametric** statistics that assume that the scores made by the respondents are distributed in a certain way. **You will even be able to use   the product moment correlation coefficient.** Constructing and using indices will be the main topic of chapter six.

Summary: What you Have Learned

We have covered a great deal in this chapter. First we considered how you should present yourself to the board to not only be authorized to do the study but even be authorized to do it on your own terms. Partly this involves being canny in self-presentation. However it also involves knowing what you are doing methodologically. You need to know why you are using probability tests, what ones are appropriate under what conditions, and why. To make you prepared we have looked at levels of measurement, revealing that most of the raw data you are with dealing represents ordinal measurement, not interval or ratio. With these data you will use nonparametric statistics, the most useful of which is chi-square. However, indices made of multiple items may give results that start to approximate a normal distribution, and may make it possible for you to use parametric statistics.

Chapter Three:
Doing a Pretest

Questionnaires and Pretests

The first step in creating your questionnaire is designing a pretest. That is what enables you to decide which items to include on the final version and what alternative answers to include in it. It is also what enables you to try out your procedures for recording and analyzing the data.

How does it differ from the final questionnaire? The main way is in its great use of open-ended questions. This is where respondents get to tell you what they want to say in response to your questions. Then it is your job to create fixed alternatives that give them a chance to say those things.

It is also where they tell you how important various issues are to them. If you have done a good job of soliciting possible questions from committees, activists, newsletters, and other sources, you should now have many more items than you will be able to use on the final questionnaire. You can have your pretest subjects answer the ones that they consider important, and skip the ones that they don't – as well as suggesting other issues that they think you should have included.

Because it is laborious for respondents to write out all of their answers this is a good place to provide some fixed alternatives but also a chance to add other answers if none of yours seems appropriate to the respondent.

Other than those differences the pretest is much like the final questionnaire. You should have enough of an idea where you are headed that you know what sections it should be divided into and where its main emphases should be. It should have some items that will be much the same on the final questionnaire, so that you can try out your data analysis techniques on them.

A hypothetical example

As an exercise let's imagine that you want to get data on an issue on which neither of us presently has any data – why the respondents chose to buy in your condominium building. Since this is a pretest you want to give them a chance to tell you in their own words. In this case that question is so central that you probably want it to come first rather than last. If it does, there is a danger of the respondents ignoring the instructions and starting to list all of the factors that were important to them. To keep them from doing that you might well want to tell them at the start that there will be other questions too.

So you might start by asking the respondent something like this: *"In this section we will be asking you a number of questions about your decision to buy here. First, would you like to tell us in your own words the most important factor leading you to do so?"*

After that, what more could you possibly ask? Actually there are several things you might consider including if you want to get all of the context:

- *What other considerations were important?*

- *Was there anyone else who was involved in the decision?*

- *If so, what were the most important factors for them?*

- *Were there reasons why you had doubts about buying?*

- *Why the other person did?*

- *Do the reasons why you bought still seem valid?*

- *Are there factors that you did not consider that you now feel should be included in such a decision?*

- *Would you make the same decision today?*

If you do ask a battery of questions such as these you will have quite a job to do in categorizing the results and writing the fixed alternatives for the final questionnaire. The responses to "*Other decision makers*" may be fairly easy to categorize – a spouse, another family member, a good friend, an expert of some kind such as a financial advisor – these are obvious categories. On the other hand the answers to the first question, "*main reason*", may be all over the map.

If you read through all of those answers and think about them, however, then certain common elements should start to emerge. Given its importance in real estate, location is bound to be prominent. How may "*location*" answers be further broken down? One distinction that may soon be obvious is that some of them deal with public factors that are the same for everyone – nearness to restaurants, cultural events, etc. Others are personal – nearness to job, relative, and so on. Gradually you will come to see the vast array of answers as variations on a limited number of themes. "*Financial*" factors will probably be common, as will specific characteristics of the "*building*" or the condo association's "*bylaws*". That the building has elevators or a swimming pool, and that its bylaws do or do not permit pets or forbid renting out your unit are all possible responses fitting in these two related categories.

Now you have gone from having too few potential fixed alternative items to having too many, so your next job is starting to pare them down. At least three things should help here: First, if you have asked the pretest respondents to comment on the questions they have been asked, then they may have given clues to the items that are important or unimportant. Second, you do not have to cover every possibility in the fixed responses if you have each set of answers accompanied by a chance to add a different one. Finally, not all respondents need to answer all questions. If each item on our original list generated a group of questions, then the respondent can skip all those groups that are not applicable. If there were no other decision makers, or the buyer had no doubts, for example, then those sections could be skipped.

You are starting to evolve a questionnaire with a section looking something like what is shown in Box III-1.

BOX III-1
How important was each of the following types of factor in the decision to buy here?

Importance → Factor ↓	VERY IM- PORTANT	IMPOR- TANT	NOT VERY IMPORTANT	NOT A FAC- TOR AT ALL
Building Location				
Financial Considera- tions				
Building Characteris- tics				
Association Bylaws				
Etc.				
Other (Please specify)				

General considerations

Studies differ greatly in the attention paid to the pretest. At one extreme are studies that simply give a few friends a copy of the proposed final questionnaire to respond to. At the other extreme are ones that recruit a diverse sample of pretest subjects, ask completely open-ended questions, and do an exhaustive study of the answers. The pretest is the first thing that is sacrificed if the research is being done under time pressure. The price that is paid is this: The less adequate job you do on the pretest, the more time you will have to spend analyzing your data at the end. With thorough pre-testing the questions on the final questionnaire will cover the things the respondents consider important and provide response categories that they find adequate. Without adequate pre-testing that will not be the case, and one of two things will result: Either you will spend a great deal of time coding respondent comments or you will not really learn what they are thinking.

Assuming that you have the time and resources to do a thorough job, here are some questions that you should ask yourself and some tentative answers. The answers are tentative because circumstances differ and you will have to decide what answer is right for your particular study.

1. Should you include the usual statement about confidentiality, given that you are working with a small group of volunteers and probably know who they are? Yes, but you should also include another question, asking them to comment on the wording of the confidentiality statement. (By now you should have decided on how you will ensure confidentiality, unless there is some extraordinary reason why it is inappropriate - and I cannot think of one.)

2. Are there any questions that you should be sure to ask on a pretest? Yes, you should ask if there are matters that you have left out that they think should be covered, unimportant ones that you have devoted too much attention to, answers to the questions that you do ask that you have forgotten to include, and general suggestions.

3. Should the preliminary questionnaire generate data for a progress report to the board? Only if they require one. Even if they do it should not cover all of the topics on the questionnaire. Instead it should show how one or two items will be analyzed, with

a caution that the results shown are by no means any indication of how things will turn out with the larger sample.

4. Given that you will have a limited number of pretest subjects and that much of what they provide will be written in their own words, is there any point in coding the responses at all? Wouldn't your time be better spent just reading and thinking about what they have written? The advantage of doing coding of the fixed alternative parts of the questionnaire is that this is your one chance to find out if there are any problems with the programs and techniques that you are going to use to get your data into usable form. You should not pass up that opportunity.

5. Are there things that you should know that you will not find out with a pretest? Yes. If you do not have a diverse enough group of participants you may not find out about inadequacies of your questions and answers. The largest area you will not find out about, however, is how adequate your procedures are for dealing with people who do not follow instructions. The volunteers who take the pretest probably will follow them. That is why you must pay particular attention to that area yourself and decide how you will code or refuse to code the answers of people who violate the instructions.

6. In what format should your questions be asked? The less your coders have to think, the better. You should therefore set up the questionnaire so that there is a separate response box for each possible answer to the question. For example, if you wanted to have the respondent give a number indicating his or her approval of a statement, then you would have to choose between having them write a number in

one box – (say a 1,2,3,4 or 5) – or having them check one box for a 1, another for a 2, and so on. The latter takes more space but is preferable.

7. Is there any particular order in which questions should be asked? There are several considerations here. First, if you are sampling more than one population, such as association members and building residents, then the questions should be divided accordingly. You might, for example, first have questions for members only, then ones for both, and finally ones for residents only. A related and obvious point is that similar questions should be put together to the extent possible. A less obvious one is this: Respondents remember best the items at the beginning and end of the questionnaire. If you ask about sensitive issues, hide those items near the middle.

8. How long should the questionnaire be? The longer it is, the fewer people who will return it and the more who will only answer some of the questions – a behavior that causes a surprising number of problems during data analysis. In cutting out items that seem to you trivial, however, be aware of an observation by organizational consultant and humorous author C. Northcote Parkinson. Parkinson noted that committees will often pass without debate items costing hundreds of thousands of dollars, then spend a long time wrangling over some trivial expense such as the amount of money spent on paper clips. The members may know nothing about the things on which the large expenditures are being made, but they know what a paper clip is. One such item in my condominium was the provision of television in the exercise room. Some residents – and I suspect there was a generational

difference here – did not know why there was an exercise room at all, while others found not having a well-equipped one as inconceivable as drinking coffee that had been brewed in a percolator. Make your decision on length, but ask pretest subjects their opinions on the matter.

9. How should the questionnaire be reproduced and distributed? As cheaply as possible. Have them printed on both sides of the page, do not use color, slip the final version under doors if possible, only paying postage for those members who do not live in the building. Following on Parkinson's observation, the members may not know how much a window-washing contract should cost but they are familiar with the cost of photocopying and mailing a document.

10. Important as those questions may be, however, there is one that comes before all the rest and is the most important of all: What analyses are you going to want to do? Failure to think this through at this point can lead, for example, to your looking into "willingness to volunteer" and deciding that you want to cross tabulate it with how long the respondent has lived in the building – only to find, OOPS, that you didn't ask about length of residence. Sit back at this point, imagine that you already have your data, and wonder – wouldn't be interesting to see if …. Then be sure to include the data *to answer that question in what you are obtaining.*

Entering the Data

Three types of spreadsheet

The first task is to read each subject's data into the computer. Whether you are extremely fortunate and can have this done by machine, such as by optical scanning, or whether a human coder has to do the job, you will probably get a spreadsheet **for each subject** that mirrors the answer sheet that he or she filled out.

For analysis you want to transfer the data from the individual subject spreadsheets into one big data matrix. "(This is the form the data will have in examples we will consider.) In other words you want to create a **databank** that contains all of your data. To doubly protect our data from unintentional change and error we will not transfer the data from the individual respondent records directly into it. Instead we will use an intermediate that we will call the **datasheet.**

So we are going to have three types of spreadsheets:

(1) The first type is the **coding sheet.** You read each questionnaire and record the answers on a copy of the coding sheet. Its format mirrors that of the questionnaire. You will open a new copy of it for each respondent, and save it as that individual's data after filling it out.

(2) Before you close the respondent's *coding sheet*, however, his or her data will be automatically transferred to the **datasheet**. Each person's data will fill one line of this sheet. The transfer occurs automatically because the coding sheet and the datasheet are **linked.** (In the next chapter you will learn how to link them.)

(3) Finally, the line of data representing that subject's data will be added to the **databank**.

When you have done those three things you will have all of the data ready to analyze.

Box III-2 shows a small portion of a ***coding sheet.*** In this case the coder usually enters an X in the appropriate box. However, one blank filled out by the respondents tells how many rental units they own. For that question the coder has to enter a number.

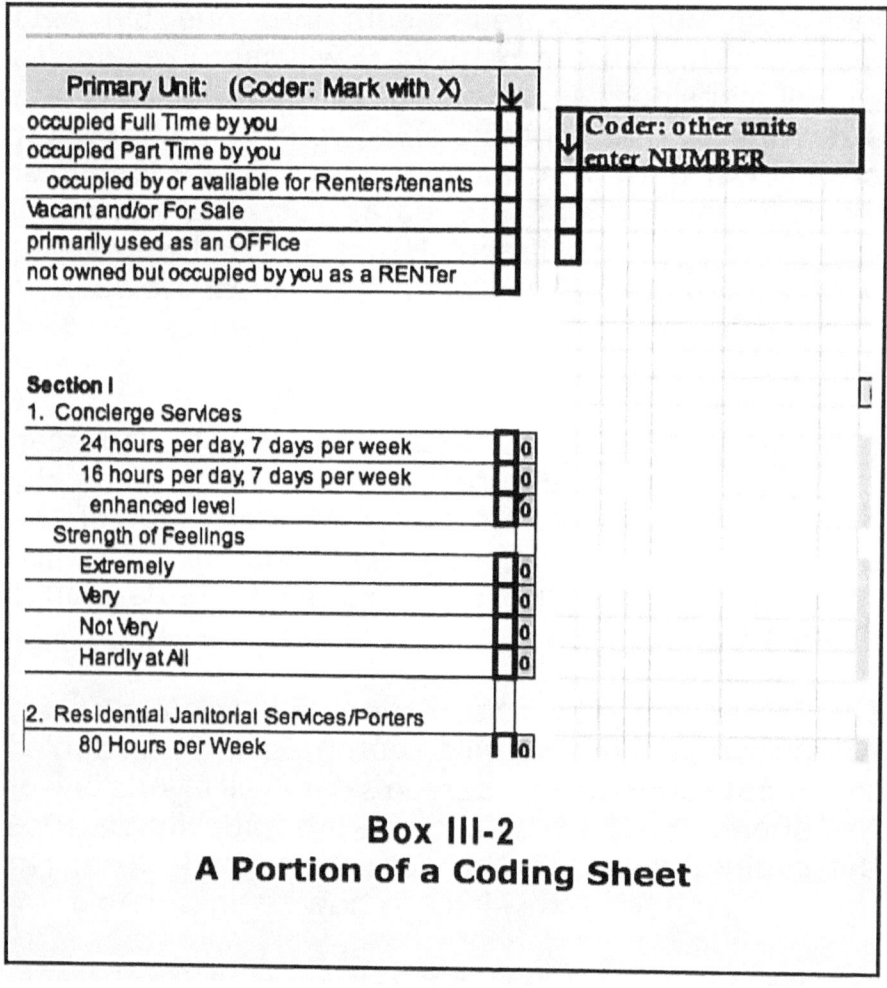

Box III-2
A Portion of a Coding Sheet

Avoiding Errors

When doing the pretest is the time to plan for how to avoid errors in recording and analyzing the data. There are number of ways in which errors may creep in:

First there is the possibility that the coding sheet is wrong, either because it was made that way initially or because it became corrupted later. It could be wrong initially if you mistakenly asked it to get the value from cell J12 when you should have said J13. You should check the results of the pretest carefully, and note any values that do not seem reasonable. To avoid any possibility of the coding sheet becoming corrupted later the original should be password protected and coders should always work with copies of the sheet, not the original.

Then there is the likely possibility that the coders will make errors. Coding is a dull job yet one that requires attention. It is easy to make errors if you work too long without a break. The work of the coders should be checked, and they should be trained until they are reliable. It may be that there is a pattern to their mistakes that it is relatively easy to overcome. When I started coding almost all of my errors were on a single item and were caused by that item's position on the questionnaire. Once this particular item was identified as the source of my errors it was easy to eliminate them.

There is another kind of error that a coder may make that can be troublesome. If the coder puts a mark on the coding sheet in almost, but not quite, the right place, then the program may not pick it up. This is one of many errors that may be avoided by building redundancy into the system. In my study I had the coder record an "X" in the box, and then the program translated it into a "1" and recorded that in the corresponding box on the right hand side of the page. Although this step was in one way unnecessary, since the coder could have recorded a 1 in the first place, it did serve a function. If the X were misplaced the coder would immediately notice that the 1 did not appear and would correct his or her error.

What happens then again illustrates the importance of not working with the master documents but copies of them. Suppose that the coder has marked cell 8M when she should have marked 9M. She notices her error and marks, 9M, removing the mark from 8M. This alone does not cure the problem, however. There is a cell, say 8T, where a 1 appeared when 8M was marked. That 1 will not be removed by removing the X from 8M. So the coder will probably remove it by hand.

That is fine if she is working with a copy of the coding sheet. A new copy will be used with each subject and the change she makes now will not affect what happens to the next subject. If she had been working with the original, however, her action would have destroyed the link that makes 8T become a 1 when 8M is marked. ALWAYS WORK WIITH A COPY, OR A READ-ONLY VERSION IF POSSIBLE.

There are many places where programming errors may be made – in transferring, manipulating, and recording the data in final form, not to mention in running the final statistical tests. Normally these are big errors that become apparent immediately. They may be less obvious, however, if they appear part way through the data recording process. That could happen, for example, if exceptional measures are being taken to correct early coding errors.

For that reason you want to limit the extent to which an error in one part is transmitted to another part. Having separate datasheet and databank helps to achieve this. The datasheet is linked to the coding sheet. When a 1 appears on the coding sheet various cells on the datasheet also change. Suppose that instead of having a separate databank you then recorded the second subject after the first one on the datasheet. You might be surprised to find that the first subject also took on the characteristics of the new one – the links would still be active. Having a separate databank is the easiest way to avoid this. You use "paste special" to paste the values from the datasheet to the databank, so that the link back to where the data came from is not transmitted. Making a mistake can only screw up the record for one subject, not all of the ones already recorded.

There are more possible sources of error than can be listed here. Hopefully you will not discover the rest of them for yourself. In any case you can at least minimize the effects of errors by doing four things:

- Use copies or read-only files where possible.

- Isolate different parts of the system from each other.

- Build redundancy into the system.

- Save your results frequently, including making backups on removable disks.

Summary

In this chapter you have learned how to do a pretest. The extent of pre-testing possible will depend on the time and resources you have available, but time spent here will be more than made up when you come to data analysis. In looking at an example you have seen how you start with general open-ended questions and use them to generate more specific ones with fixed alternatives in the final questionnaire. You have also seen how the pretest gives you a chance to check out your procedures and avoid errors later.

Chapter Four:
Introduction to Data Analysis

Examining a spreadsheet

As you continue with developing your questionnaire there are many decisions that you will have to make. Your decisions will partly depend on the size of your group and the resources you have available. Should you be surveying a small association you might want to use open-ended questions where the respondents answer in their own words. With enough coders that might be feasible. Usually it is better to have fixed alternatives. Coding the responses is one of the largest jobs, unless you have the resources to have the responses machine read. To make the decisions that you face at this point you must know just how the spreadsheet works

A real life example. In Box IV-1 we have a typical bit of a spreadsheet. Each of the rows represents the record from one subject. There are only nine of them in this example, numbered down the left. The labels at the bottom tell what the columns mean. A "1" in a cell means that thing applies to that subject. A "0" means that it doesn't. Looking at column B, for example, we find that only one of the nine subjects wanted a security patrol 12 times per day.

A	B	C	D	E	F	G	H	I	J	K	L	M	N	O	P
1	0	1	0	0	1	0	0	0	0	1	0	0	0	1	0
2	0	0	0	0	0	0	0	0	0	0	0	0	0	0	0
3	1	0	0	0	1	0	0	0	1	0	0	0	0	0	1
4	0	0	1	0	0	1	0	0	0	1	0	0	1	0	0
5	0	1	0	0	0	1	0	0	1	0	0	1	0	0	0
6	0	0	0	0	0	0	0	0	0	0	0	0	0	0	0
7	0	1	0	0	1	0	0	0	1	0	0	1	0	0	0
8	0	1	0	0	1	0	0	0	1	0	0	1	0	0	0
9	0	0	0	1	1	0	0	0	0	1	0	0	0	1	0

Column headers (B–P):
- B: Patrol 12 times per day
- C: patrol 7 times per day
- D: patrol 4 times per day
- E: enhanced security patrols
- F: Patrol Feel extremely
- G: Patrol Feel very strongly
- H: Patrol Feel not v. strongly
- I: Patrol Feel hardly at all
- J: Windows 4 times per year
- K: Windows 3 times per year
- L: Windows 2 times per year
- M: Windows Feel extremely
- N: Windows Feel v. strongly
- O: Windows Not very strongly
- P: Windows Feel hardly at all

BOX IV-1.
A portion of a spreadsheet.

As we continue examining the data, however, we notice one anomaly. Columns B, C, and D represent the three possible answers to the question about security. Each person should have picked one of them. What about the three people who did not mark in column B, C, or D – that is, did not indicate any number of times that the security patrol should come around? Respondent #2 probably was a renter, since renters did not fill out the part of the questionnaire represented by columns B through U but did fill out the ones after that. (Later portions of this subject's spreadsheet, not shown here, show that the subject did have answers after column U.) Respondent #6 seems to have been one of the very small group who turned in mostly blank questionnaires. Record #9 may actually represent a coding error, for these are the records before they were checked for errors. When they were, quite a few errors had to be corrected in the early records.

If we were actually in a spreadsheet program you would be able to highlight a column or row with a single click. To highlight column G, for example, you would just click on the letter G. To highlight a row you would click on its number.

Since we are not in a spreadsheet program, however, our first exercise will have to be a thought experiment. Here is our first magic trick:

(1) Highlight the empty square just below the numbers in column B.

(2) Then look at the various things shown in the toolbar across the top of the spreadsheet and find an "add up" (or "sum" symbol: Σ.)

(3)Click on it.

(4) What you get is a message asking if you want to sum the column. What is to be summed is shown in two ways, by the box around the figures and by the notation "B1:B9" which means cells B1 through B9. **Pressing "return" is all the answer you need give**. Do so and the sum of column B will appear at the foot of the numbers – in this case the not very exciting answer of "1."

These steps are shown in Boxes IV-2 through IV-4

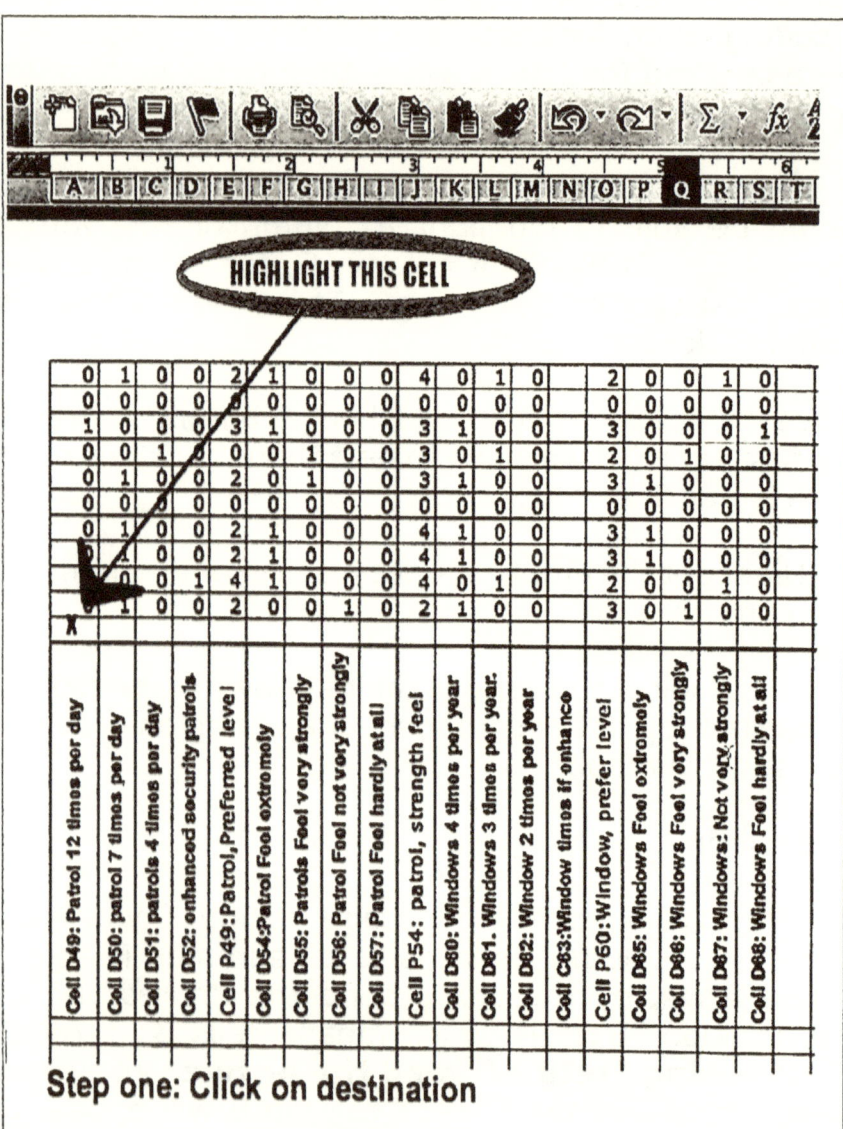

Step one: Click on destination

BOX IV-2.

First step in inserting a function

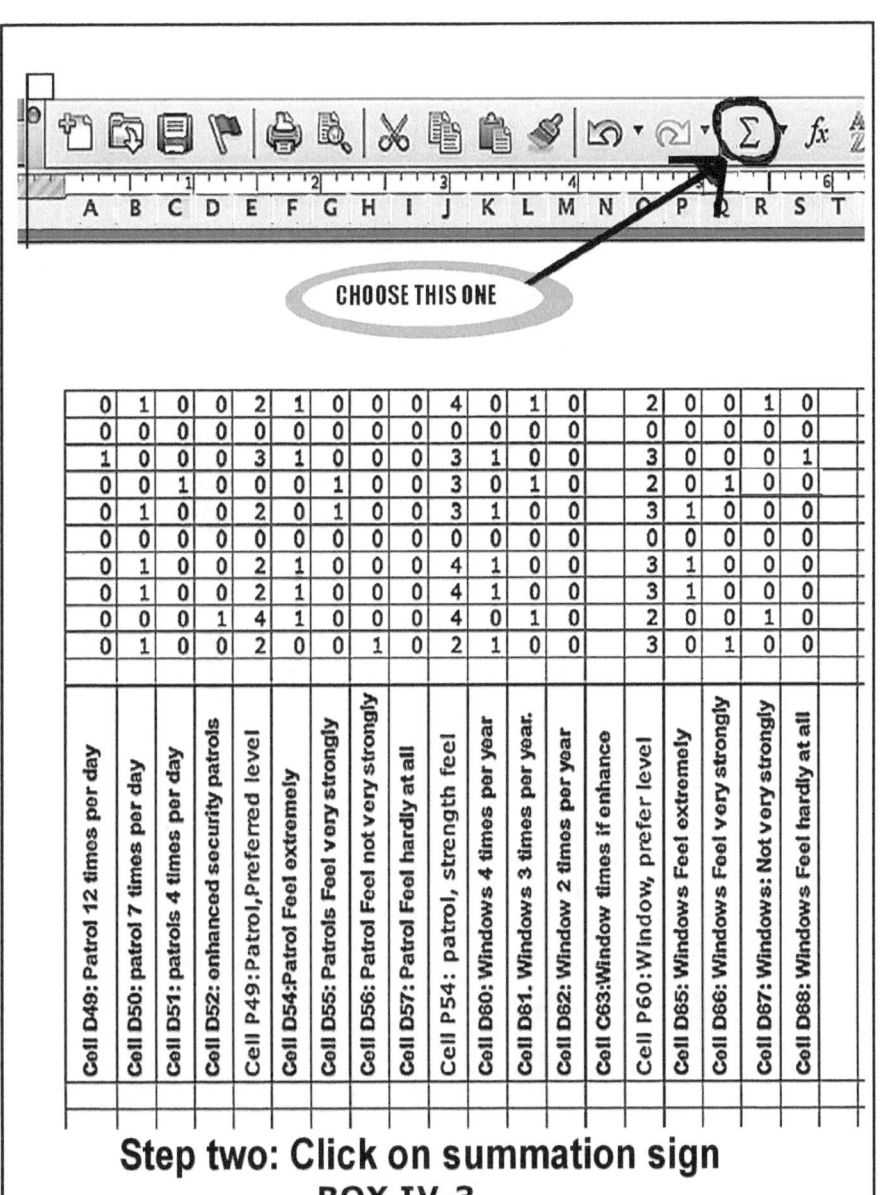

Cell D49: Patrol 12 times per day	Cell D50: patrol 7 times per day	Cell D51: patrols 4 times per day	Cell D52: enhanced security patrols	Cell P49:Patrol,Preferred level	Cell D54:Patrol Feel extremely	Cell D55: Patrols Feel very strongly	Cell D56: Patrol Feel not very strongly	Cell D57: Patrol Feel hardly at all	Cell P54: patrol, strength feel	Cell D60: Windows 4 times per year	Cell D81. Windows 3 times per year.	Cell D62: Window 2 times per year	Cell C63:Window times if enhance	Cell P60:Window, prefer level	Cell D65: Windows Feel extremely	Cell D66: Windows Feel very strongly	Cell D67: Windows: Not very strongly	Cell D88: Windows Feel hardly at all
0	1	0	0	2	1	0	0	0	4	0	1	0		2	0	0	1	0
0	0	0	0	0	0	0	0	0	0	0	0	0		0	0	0	0	0
1	0	0	0	3	1	0	0	0	3	1	0	0		3	0	0	0	1
0	0	1	0	0	0	1	0	0	3	0	1	0		2	0	1	0	0
0	1	0	0	2	0	1	0	0	3	1	0	0		3	1	0	0	0
0	0	0	0	0	0	0	0	0	0	0	0	0		0	0	0	0	0
0	1	0	0	2	1	0	0	0	4	1	0	0		3	1	0	0	0
0	1	0	0	2	1	0	0	0	4	1	0	0		3	1	0	0	0
0	0	0	1	4	1	0	0	0	4	0	1	0		2	0	0	1	0
0	1	0	0	2	0	0	1	0	2	1	0	0		3	0	1	0	0

CHOOSE THIS ONE

Step two: Click on summation sign
BOX IV-3
Second step in inserting a function

And here is what you get.

	Patrol 12 times per day	patrol 7 times per day	patrols 4 times per day	enhanced security patrols	Patrol Feel extremely	Patrols Feel very strongly	Patrol Feel not very strongly	Patrol Feel hardly at all
1	0	1	0	0	1	0	0	0
2	0	0	0	0	0	0	0	0
3	1	0	0	0	1	0	0	0
4	0	0	1	0	0	1	0	0
5	0	1	0	0	0	1	0	0
6	0	0	0	0	0	0	0	0
7	0	1	0	0	1	0	0	0
8	0	1	0	0	1	0	0	0
9	0	0	0	1	1	0	0	0
=SUM(B1:B9)								

Box IV-4
Third step in inserting a function

To review, what you have done is to add up column B. By clicking in the cell at the foot of the column you told the summation process that it was column B you want to add up. When you clicked on the summation sign it asked you if that were the case, as is shown in Box IV-4.

The program assumed that you wanted to add up the numbers above the cell that you highlighted on before clicking on the summation sign. You may want the sum to appear in some other place, however. Here is how you do that: You can highlight the place you want it to appear, click on the summation sign, ignore what the program highlights, highlight the column you want to sum, and hit "return." The program will put the sum in the destination you have chosen. Note: do not hit "return" until you have instructed the program what cells you want added up and where to put the sum.

When you pressed "return" it added up the column and put the result in the cell you had highlighted at the start.

It probably won't happen the first time you do this, but at some point you will get the message " It looks like you are managing a list, would you like the help of the list manager?" If you get this message click on the appropriate box for telling the machine to butt out and resume where you were when you were so rudely interrupted. The list manager is one of many subprograms in your machine that try to think for you. Often they are helpful or even essential. Frequently they guess wrong about what you are trying to do and are no help at all. Because of this we must digress for a moment.

One of the most maddening things about either writing or following instructions is that the expected thing sometimes does not happen. For the person following the instructions what happens is that you perform one step and then the option you are supposed to pick next isn't there to pick. For the person writing the instructions it is as if one were trying to tell someone how to fix their car without knowing what kind of car they own. There are a number of spreadsheet programs and they are revised from time to time. My instructions on how to adjust the carburetor will not work if you have fuel injection.

The relevance of this is that the list manager may have been active and decided that it is not B1 thru B9 that you want to sum but some other combination of numbers. If so those will be the ones that it highlights. You can ignore this and highlight the ones that you really want. It is the action of hitting "return" that tells the program to proceed with the addition. Don't hit "return" until the right things are highlighted. When we highlight something it makes the program's highlighting go away.

That the list manager may intrude itself is a heck of a note when you are just getting started and I am trying to keep it simple. However you can learn something from it. When the instructions don't work, not just here but any time, you have to be bold and try to figure out what does. To keep from losing all your work while playing around, do not work with the original of your data set. Copy it and work with the copy, only updating the master version when you know that what you have done is the right thing. They say that nothing you do to your computer is likely to do permanent damage other than dropping it on the floor or spilling liquid on it, so if problems arise use a *copy and go to it. In computer work, as in life, half of it is just showing up - in this case being willing to try things.*

Now let's hope that there was no complication in your following these first instructions. If it didn't happen this time, however, remember that it is sure to sooner or later.

Working with Functions

Returning to the main theme we see that what you have accomplished so far is to get the sum of a column of numbers. That is not all you have accomplished, however. What you have also done is to **insert a function,** tell it what **parameters** to use, and **carry out the calculation.**

Inserting functions is one of the main things you will be doing in analyzing data. **A *function* (abbreviated *f*) is essentially an instruction to do a certain thing to a number or numbers.** The function that you used was "sum," (abbreviated **Σ**). It is an instruction to add up the numbers. "Take the square of", "take the square root of", "copy the smallest of the bunch", and "calculate the sum of the ones larger than 3" are all functions. So is "copy the number that is in the cell on the same line as this one but in column R."

The **parameters** are the values to be used by the **function**, in this case the numbers in cells B1 thru B9. Each function that you insert asks you what set or sets of numbers you want to use in its calculation. If you are doing a sum it asks you what numbers you want summed. If you are doing $\Sigma(X^2 + Y^2)$ it will ask you what X's and Y's to use. In our first example the program did some thinking for you – hopefully, correctly. When you put the summation sign at the bottom of the column of figures it assumed that those figures were what you wanted to add up. We have just seen how you deal with it when that is not the case.

Let's look at a different way that you can carry out the function. You start in the same way by highlighting the destination cell where you want the sum to appear. Instead of clicking on the summation sign at the top of the page, however, you go to the "insert" column and click on "function." This opens up a very long list of functions that you could use. When you click on "sum" it opens a box asking you what you want to sum. You indicate the column of cells by giving the address of the first one (such as B1) followed by a colon and the address of the last one (such as B9.) When you click on "OK" the function is applied

An example of a function insertion box is given in Box IV-5. The word "sum" at the upper left tells what **function** is to be carried out. The boxes are where you indicate the **parameters** - the numbers to be added. (As each box is filled another one appears in case you have more numbers to add.) When you click on "OK" the function is carried out – in this case adding eight zeros and a one to get one. **Especially note** the question mark in the lower left corner of the function insertion box. If you click on it you will be taken to a detailed description of how the function works, with examples.

```
┌─────────────────────────────────────────────────────────┐
│                                                           │
│  SUM                                                      │
│  ─────────────────────────────────────────────────       │
│     Number1  │ B1:B9│        │ ▲ │  =  {0;0;1;0;0;0;0;0;0} │
│                                                           │
│     Number2  │         │     │ ▲ │  =  number             │
│                                                           │
│                                          =  1             │
│                                                           │
│  Adds all the numbers in a range of cells.                │
│                                                           │
│       Number1:  number1,number2,... are 1 to 30 numbers to sum. Logical values │
│                 and text are ignored in cells, included if typed as arguments. │
│                                                           │
│  │?│  Formula result =  1              ( Cancel ) ( OK )  │
│                                                           │
└─────────────────────────────────────────────────────────┘
```

Box IV-5
A function insertion box

Before we leave this example there is one more magic trick that we should do. Look way back where the spreadsheet was first presented, with data in columns B thru P. You used a function to sum column B. Now we are going to use it to sum all the other columns at one fell swoop. We will do that by using the "copy" function, remembering that it will apply the summation function to the other columns of numbers rather than just copying the sum of column B:

- (In your imagination) highlight the sum of Column B.

- Then on the "edit" menu click on "copy."

- Now highlight cells C10 thru P10. (You do this by holding down the mouse button while moving from C10 to P10 or vice versa, then releasing the mouse button.)

- After that select "paste" from the edit menu and release the mouse button while "paste" is selected.

That exercise illustrated a point that cannot be overemphasized: . When you had the program copy cell B10 it did not copy the number that was there but rather did the same thing to the other columns that it had done to column B. It did not copy a "1" into each cell, but what it got by applying the "sum" function to each new column of numbers.

If you had wanted it to copy the number instead you would have selected "paste special" from the edit menu instead of "paste." That would have opened a dialogue box where you would have clicked on "value": and then clicked "OK."

Digression: Linking Spreadsheets

In the last chapter I promised that this one would tell you how to link spreadsheets. The time to do that has now come. You will need to do this to link the CODING SHEET where the coder records the data from each subject, the DATASHEET where each person's data are put on a single line, and the DATABANK where all the subjects are combined.

Look back at Box IV-1. Let's imagine that it is a part of a spreadsheet called "Pretest." Let's open it in our spreadsheet program. Leaving it open, but moving in its edges so that it does not take the entire screen, let's also have the program open a new blank spreadsheet.

When it does so you will find that the columns are much wider than the ones we have been dealing with. At the top of the page click on "format" and then choose "column." Under column select "standard width" and set it at about 0.4" That is a value that gives you columns that are wide enough to work with but do not take up so much space that the spreadsheet becomes huge. If you prefer to make them a bit wider or narrower feel free to do so. Save the new spreadsheet under some name that is meaningful, such as "Number Two," but do not close it.

First let's transfer a single cell. Choose a destination cell in "Number Two" and click on it. Then type "=" on your keyboard. Click on the cell in "Pretest" that you want copied to Number Two and press "return." The program will describe where that source cell is, but you do not need to pay attention to that. The important thing is that the future value of the cell in "Pretest" now appears in the location you have chosen for it in "Number Two."

From now on, whenever you open "Number Two" it will ask you what you want to do about its link to "Pretest." You can choose to ignore the link so that the value of the cell in "Number Two" will be unchanged. Or you can choose to open "Pretest" so that it can make the transfer. Finally, you can choose to cut the link. If you do this it will be gone forever, just as if it had never existed.

Now that you know how to link two spreadsheets you are ready to make the **datasheet** for your study. You will remember that when the coders record each respondent's answers on the **coding sheet** they fall all over that sheet. There is an entire sheet for each person. To analyze the data, however, we want each person's data to fall on a single line of a spreadsheet. The links between the coding sheet and the datasheet make up a template to achieve that.

Because the first item on the datasheet may come, for example, from C8 on the coding sheet, and the second one may come from R1 or H14 or whatever, it is obvious that the links between coding sheet and datasheet must be forged one by one. That means, however, that you already know how to make the datasheet. All you do is make a link between the first space on the datasheet and the place on the coding sheet where you will find that information. Then you do so for what you want in the second space of the row and so on until you are done. When a respondent's data are transferred that subject will occupy only one row. When the rows are all combined they will make up the databank.

If you want to label the datasheet to remind yourself what is in each cell the spreadsheet program has a way to do this. Go to "cell" in the format column and explore the possibilities.

It is a good thing that you only have to make the datasheet once, rather than making new links to transfer the data on each respondent!

Now the good news is that there **is** an easy way to set up the transfer from your datasheet to your databank, for there you are transferring a row of values to a similar position in their new home. After setting up your datasheet you can simply highlight the row of cells representing one subject and select "copy" from the menu. Then highlight a row in a blank spreadsheet.

Now you probably expect me to say that you should then select "paste." Instead I am going to tell you to select "paste special" and then "values." If you did not do that, your entering the next subject's data would change this subject's entries to correspond to those, for the link would still be active. As its name says, "values" pastes the current number in each cell, not a formula to keep revising the numbers as those on the source sheet change.

Procedures like the ones described in this section probably seem quite alien to you now. They will soon become second nature, for you will be repeating them very many times.

Other useful functions

There are many other functions in your spreadsheet program ready for you to use. So far you have seen how to transfer the contents of cells and use the function "**sum.**" Other useful functions are "**sum if**", "**count,**" "**count if,**" and "**if.**"

Useful as "sum" is, it is less so than "sum if." "Sum if" only adds numbers if they meet a condition that you specify. You can specify that a number only be added if it is >0 (greater than zero), or <29 (less than 29), or whatever restriction you want. What makes the function really powerful, however, is that the condition does not have to be some characteristic of the number to be added. **It can be a characteristic of what is**

in some other cell. You just have to specify what other cell.

Consider this typical example: Perhaps in column H you have recorded whether the respondent is male or female. In column AR you have recorded whether they are very concerned about security. You want to compare the proportion of males and females that are very concerned about that issue. With "sum if" you can tell the program to add the number in column AR only if the entry on that line in column H is "male." Then you could do the same with "female." That is shown in Box IV-6.

Males (H=0)	$\sum$ AR if H=0: males concerned about security 27	(62) minus (number at left): males unconcerned with security = 35	Number males = 62
Females (H=1)	$\sum$ AR if H=1: females concerned about security 50	(80) minus (number at left): females unconcerned with security = 30	Number females= 80
	AR=1 concerned about security	AR=0 unconcerned about security	↑ Row totals
Column totals➜	Number concerned about security = 77	Number unconcerned with security = 65	N = 142 total respon- dents

BOX IV-6
Numbers of men & women concerned about security (hypothetical data)

Let's look at table IV-6 and see where the numbers came from. As I have already mentioned, the figure in the upper left hand box can be generated by using "sum if." The program is told to only sum people concerned about safety (column AR) if they are male (column H.) The number in the lower left hand box is generated in the same way, with the program told to only sum the numbers for females.

In this example I have shown two numbers generated by subtraction. The number of males unconcerned about safety is the total number of males minus the number of them who are concerned about safety. The number of females in the lower right hand box was generated in the same way.

Actually you would only have to use "sum if" to generate the number in one of the boxes. Knowing that one, and the column and row totals you could get the others. (Remember what I said earlier about there being more than one way to solve a problem?) We will return to this example in the next chapter.

Summary

In this chapter you have learned about working with spreadsheets. You have learned how the data are represented in them, and how you can manipulate the data by using functions. In the next chapter you will learn how to do two significance tests.

Extended Development – Exercises

It has reached the point where it would be difficult for you to learn any more about spreadsheets without practicing with one. There are many data sets available on the web. (If the one I mention is no longer available Google will find you many more.) Let's try this one:

http://mathforum.org/workshops/sum96/data. collections/datalibrary/data.set6.html

Go there and click on "1984-1993 Teen Statistics". Open the file in your spreadsheet program and try doing these things: sum a column of numbers, sum it using "sum if" and setting a condition applying to that column, do that again by setting a condition applying to some other column, click on "insert function" and look at all the functions available to you. Pick a couple at random and see what they do...When you have fooled around with the numbers until you are confident in what you are doing you will have mastered working with spreadsheets, never mind what you have learned about surveying attitudes.

Chapter Five:
Running Statistical Tests

This chapter and the one after it are the ones that are heaviest on statistics. In this one we look in detail at chi-square since it is the test you will be using when you have ordinal data. In the next chapter we consider the question of when you can use parametric tests, and show analyses using them.

Nonparametric: chi-square

Chi-square works by comparing what you observe with what you expect. Suppose that you are suspicious of a pair of dice. You roll them five times in a row and get a seven every time. You do not need to be a statistician to conclude that this is unlikely to happen by chance. It differs very much from what you would **expect** – that you would get a seven about one roll in 6. In fact the run of sevens that you observed passes our criterion for being extremely significant, for it would happen less often than one time in a thousand by chance.

Expected frequencies. Suppose that there have quite a few complaints in your condo building about noisy parties. They seem to occur especially on the first and second floors. There are twenty floors, yet 5 of the 10 noisy parties occurred on the first or second floor. If there is no real relationship between elevation and having noisy parties, could these **observed** values have occurred by chance?

To answer this question we have to compare the number that did occur there with the number that we would **expect** to occur there. Floors 1& 2 make up one-tenth of the building. If there were no relationship between floor and whooping it up we would expect that on average there would be one noisy party there out of ten rather than five. The expected number of noisy parties is the proportion of the floors involved (1/10) times the number of parties. Calculating the expected frequency in this example – (a single case) - is simple and obvious. (We will return to this example in a little while.)

A More Complex Case. Now let us consider a more complicated example by looking at the data in Box V-1. It shows the relationship between average per capita income and average family income for fifty communities. In general the families with high per capita income also have high family income. The two variables are not perfectly correlated, however. Perhaps the communities differ in what proportion of their families have multiple wage earners.

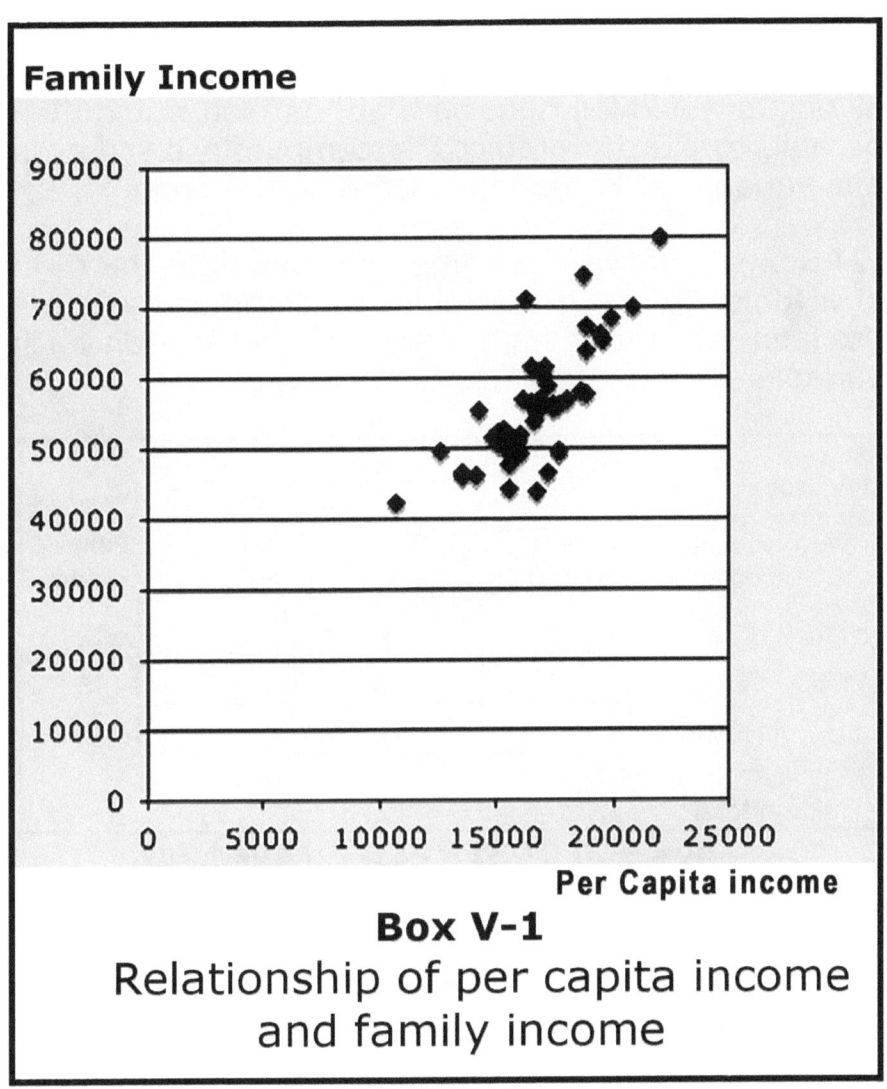

Family Income

Box V-1
Relationship of per capita income
and family income

The *observed* relationship between the two variables
is shown in Boxes V-1 and V-2 in two ways:

(1) Box V-1 is a *scatter plot*. Each community
is represented by a dot, with the height of the dot
indicating average family income and how far it is
to the right indicating the community's average per
capita income. The tendency of the dots to fall along

a diagonal line indicates the correlation between the variables. If the two variables were perfectly correlated all points would fall right on that line: You would then be able to exactly predict the community's score on one variable by knowing its score on the other.

(2) Box V-2 shows the same information in the form of a table. To make the table the communities were grouped into those high, medium, and low on each variable.

per capita income ↓ / family income →	Low, <50,000	50,000-60,000	High, >60,000	Row totals:
High, >18,000	0	3	9	12
16,000-18,000	4	10	4	18
Low, <16,000	10	10	0	20
Column totals	14	23	13	N=50

Box V-2. OBSERVED Frequencies:
Apparent Relationship

In the table as in the scatter plot you can see the relationship between the two variables. Think about what correlation is: Positive correlation means that high scores on one variable go with high scores on the other one, and low scores are similarly related. That is just what we see in table V-2: There are high frequencies in cells where both variables are high or both are low, and no cases where one is very high and the other is very low. High per capita income and high family income do seem to go along together. The question is, is it probable that a relationship this strong in the sample would occur by chance if the two variables were not in fact correlated in the population from which the sample was drawn? That is the question that our statistical test will answer.

Calculating expected frequencies

Let's show what you might expect if they were unrelated. To do this we will draw up a table similar to the one above but with the numbers indicating how many cases we would **expect** to fall in each cell. (We will let the numbers be fractional even though they couldn't have been in reality. This is one of those illogical-seeming things that we just have to accept. At least the ones here are fewer and less mind-boggling than they would be if we were talking about quantum mechanics.)

Let's look first at the upper left hand cell of our new table. To calculate how many cases we would expect to fall in that cell we reason thus: (1) We have a total of 50 cases. (2) 20 cases, or 40 % of the total, have low individual incomes. (3) In general 28% of our sample have low family incomes. (4) What proportion of the 20 cases with low individual income would we expect to also have low family income? Why, 28%. If there were no relationship between the two variables the proportion with low family income would be the same for all individual income groups. (5) So we would expect the number of communities that would have both low family and low individual income to be 28% of 40% of 50. (6) That is 5.6 cases.

Stated as simply as possible, **the expected frequency in any cell is its "row total" times its "column total" divided by the total number of cases, N.**

For example, consider the middle cell – the communities that are average on both variables. That cell's row total is 18, its column total is 23, and the number of cases is 50. The expected frequency for that cell is 18X23÷50=8.28

Using the row totals and column totals from Box V-2, we get the expected frequencies shown in Box V-3.

per capita income ↓ / family income →	<50,000	50,000-60,000	>60,000	Row Totals
>18,000	3.36	5.52	3.12	12
16,000-18000	5.04	8.28	4.68	18
<16,000	5.6	9.2	5.2	20
Column totals	14	23	13	50

Box V-3. Expected Frequencies.

These are the values we would expect, on average, if the variables had been unrelated. Whether per capita income is high, low, or medium would then have no effect on whether the other variable was high, low, or medium.

Now you have what you need to run chi-square. You input the observed and expected frequencies into your computer and in a fraction of a second it will give you the probability that the results you observed could be due to chance.

Boxes V-2 and V-3 have the information needed to run the chi square. Here is how you do it:

1.   Open a blank spreadsheet and copy the two tables onto it.
2.   Put the cursor on the cell where you want to have the probability value appear. (Be sure that it is

reasonably wide - 8 spaces or more – or the program will truncate the answer to fit the space. You can change its width by going to "column width" under "format.")

3.   Select "insert function" and choose "chitest." A function instruction box will pop up on the spreadsheet.

4.   On the function instruction box click on the space after "Actual_Range."

5.   Holding down the mouse button, run the cursor over the 9 main cells of Box V-2.

6.   On the function instruction box click on the space after "Expected_Range."

7.   Again holding down the mouse button run the cursor over the 9 main cells of Box V-3. Be sure to go over them in the same order as in step 5.

8.   When you click on "OK" the result will appear in the box that you highlighted at the start.

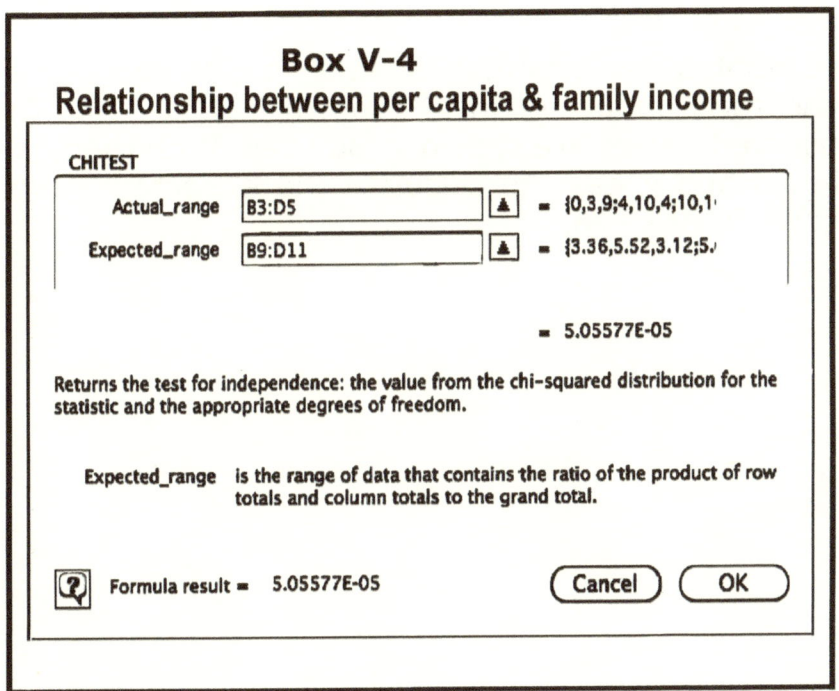

Box V-4
Relationship between per capita & family income

CHITEST

| Actual_range | B3:D5 | ▲ | = {0,3,9;4,10,4;10,1 |
| Expected_range | B9:D11 | ▲ | = {3.36,5.52,3.12;5. |

= 5.05577E-05

Returns the test for independence: the value from the chi-squared distribution for the statistic and the appropriate degrees of freedom.

Expected_range   is the range of data that contains the ratio of the product of row totals and column totals to the grand total.

Formula result = 5.05577E-05   Cancel   OK

77

In Box V-4 you can see the function instruction box for these data as it will appear just before you click on "OK." The probability is already shown as "formula result," all ready to be transferred to the chosen cell on the spreadsheet. Note that the probability is in scientific notation. Since there is a minus after the E, you should move the decimal 5 places to the left. The results would occur by chance less than one time in ten thousand.

Of course you will not be comparing individual and family income. You will instead be looking at such things as whether resident owners and non-resident ones differ in their preferences, and what factors influence whether or not a person favors buying more equipment for the exercise room. Whatever differences you observe you can test whether or not they are significant by using chi-square.

Another example.

Remember our hypothetical data on men and women concerned about security? (shown in box IV-6) Our observed values are shown in Box V-5. With them you should find it easy to calculate the expected values, shown in Box V-6.

concern gender	concerned security	unconcerned security	row totals
males	27	35	62
females	50	30	80
column totals	77	65	N= 142

Box V-5.
Observed values on concern about security (hypothetical)

concern gender	concerned security	unconcerned security	row totals
males	33.62	28.38	62
females	43.38	36.62	80
column totals	77	65	N= 142

Box V-6.
Expected values on concern about security

If we ran a chi-square on these data we would get a probability value of .02455

Extended Development – Yates' Correction

There is one more thing that you will have to know about chi-square before you actually do your data analysis. When the number of cases is very small a single case can have an inordinate effect. You need to deal with that in two ways: (1) If the number of cases is too small you simply can't use the test. (2) If you can use the test you apply a correction to keep from overestimating the significance of the data.

Let us look at those two rules by returning to the question of the noisy parties. You will remember that there were ten parties generating complaints last year, and five of them were on floor one or floor two of your twenty-story building. Those floors are just one-tenth of the building, yet half the noisy parties were there. The question we are asking is whether this is just chance, or whether there is some real relationship between living near the ground level and partying.

We start by drawing up tables of observed and expected frequencies following the procedures we have just been considering. They are shown in Box V-7.

Box V-7.

Floors 1 & 2	5 noisy parties
Floors 3-20	5 noisy parties

Observed party distribution.

Floors 1 & 2	1 noisy parties
Floors 3-20	9 noisy parties

Expected party distribution.

There is a very good reason why we should not run a chi-square analysis on these data: You should never do a chi-square analysis on data if any cell has an expected value **of less than five.** (You would be able to do a test on these data using a test we will discuss in the next chapter, one based on the binomial expansion.)

Now let's consider a case where you could use chi-square. Imagine that your condo has a great deal of trouble with noisy parties. There have been 60 of them in the last year, thirty of them on floors 1 and 2. Now our observed and expected frequencies are as shown in Box V-8.

Box V-8

Floors 1 & 2	30 noisy parties
Floors 3-20	30 noisy parties

New observed party distribution.

Floors 1 & 2	6 noisy parties
Floors 3-20	54 noisy parties

New expected party distribution.

One cell still has a pretty low expected value, even though it is over five. When numbers are this small a correction is done that reduces the probability of the results being significant. It asks, would your results still be significant even if the expected numbers had been a little more like the observed ones than they are? Would they still be significant if you had expected 6.5 noisy parties on the first two floor and 53.5 on the ones above?

So we arbitrarily change our expected values by .5 each, making each of them that much closer to the ones that were observed. That is **Yates' correction,** and we will use it to err on the side of being conservative in assessing significance. Here it is applied to the matter of the noisy parties. The expected value in the top cell was smaller than the observed value, so we increased the expected value by .5 The value in the bottom cell was larger than the observed value so we reduced it by .5 The result is shown in Box V-9. The results would occur just over 1 time in a billion by chance.

Box V-9. Corrected expected party distribution.	
Floors 1 & 2	**6.5 noisy parties**
Floors 3-20	**53.5 noisy parties**

And here in Box V-10 is what we get as our table of expected values on the **income analysis** above if we apply Yates' correction to it.

per capita income ↓ /family income→	Low, <50,000	50,000-60,000	High, >60,000	Row totals:
High, >18,000	2.86	5.52	3.62	12
16,000-18,000	5.04	8.28	4.68	18
Low, <16,000	6.10	9.2	4.7	20
Column totals	14	23	13	N=50

Box V-10. Revised table of expected values

You will note that two of the cells have expected frequencies under five. If we were actually going to do this analysis we would change our category boundaries, perhaps making our highest per capita income category start at $17,500 instead of $18,000 and our lowest per capita income category start at 16,300 instead of 16,000. That would give us higher expected frequencies in the cells that are now under 5. However, since we have gone this far let's see what the probability level **would have been** if the analysis had been justified.

Calculating chi-square we find the data would have been extremely significant, occurring less than one time in a thousand by chance.

Summary

In this chapter we have run a number of analyses using chi-square. By now you should know how to calculate expected frequencies, when it is or isn't appropriate to use the statistic, and how to apply Yates' correction when doing so is necessary. This material, combined with that in the previous chapter on how to get the data into usable form, should make you thoroughly prepared for running significance tests on your ordinal data.

Chapter Six:
Parametric Statistics

Two Laws of Probability

There are two basic laws of probability. Both of them deal with things that either happen or they don't. You either roll a 12 on the dice or you don't. The party is either on one of the first two floors or it isn't. The possibilities are thus mutually exclusive – the party cannot simultaneously be on the first two floors and not on the first two floors. And in the cases that we will be considering they are also independent – what you roll the second time you roll the dice is uninfluenced by what you rolled the first time. To such events these rules apply:

1.   If there are two **mutually exclusive** things that can happen to something, the probability that **one or the other** of them will happen is the **sum** of their individual probabilities. If you draw a card from a deck, its being a club, diamond, heart, or spade are mutually exclusive. Each time you draw it will be one of those four things, and cannot be more than one of them. The probability you will draw a spade is .25 The probability that you will draw a club is .25 In the long run the probability that you will draw a black card is the sum of those – it will happen half the time. That does not predict what will happen on any particular draw. Probabilities deal with what happens in the long run. They do not predict particular events.

2.   If there are two possible **independent** events, such as my having a

ticket to a play and it raining on any particular evening, then the probability that **both** of them will happen at once is the **product** of their individual probabilities. If I have a ticket to a play on average once every forty days (P=.025) and it rains one fifth of the evenings (P=.20), then the probability that I will both have a ticket to a play and it will rain that evening is .025X.20 = .005 In the long run both events will occur at once only about five times in a thousand days, or not quite twice a year. .

(If you apply these principles to poker you will see why it is generally unwise to draw to an inside straight.)

The Binomial Expansion

Those general rules of probability make possible a very useful statistical test, one based on what you get if one event has a probability p, and the other has probability 1-p and you raise the binomial (p)+ (1-p) to successively higher powers. The **binomial distribution test** can tell you the probability of getting a certain outcome in a given number of trials –such as getting seven heads in ten flips of a coin.

Let's consider what those two starting probabilities mean. It means that we are dealing with two **mutually exclusive** events where the two are the **only things that can happen.** Either it rains or it doesn't. Either the dice sum to seven or they don't. If the probability of it raining is .3 then the probability of it not raining is .7 The two probabilities sum to one, for one or the other must happen,

With numbers like that, if something happens a given number of times in a certain number of trials, the binomial expansion tells you the probability of that happening by chance. Let's consider something we briefly referred to earlier and one that seems very unlikely to occur by chance – the possibility that someone can roll five 7's in a row with a pair of dice.

Here the given number of times is five – the person rolls five sevens. The certain number of trials is also five – they do it in five rolls of the dice.

Each time that he or she rolls a seven we will count that as a success. Let's see just how unlikely it is that the person can have five successes in a row. The binomial distribution can give us the answer. (See Box VI-1.)

BINOMDIST

Number_s	5	▲	= 5
Trials	5	▲	= 5
Probability_s	.16667	▲	= 0.16667
Cumulative	FALSE	▲	= FALSE

= 0.000128614

Returns the individual term binomial distribution probability.

Cumulative Is a logical value: for the cumulative distribution function, use TRUE; for the probability mass function, use FALSE.

Formula result = 0.000128614   Cancel   OK

Box VI-1. Binomial function insertion box

Box VI-1 shows the "binomdist" function of the spreadsheet. The first row asks for the number of successes, in this case 5 for rolling five sevens. The second row asks how many trials those successes were achieved in, in this case also five. The third row asks the overall probability, (p), of a success on any one trial, which is one in six or .1 followed by 6 recurring, (a string of sixes stretching to infinity.) Running the binomial function tells us that the odds against such a feat happening by chance are very long. It would happen only a bit over one time in ten thousand by chance. (p=0.000128614) That figure is shown on the binomial function insertion box, (Box VI-1.)

The last line of the function insertion box says "cumulative", and is sometimes a bit tricky, as we shall see in a moment. It asks whether you want the probability of a single specified outcome - in this case exactly five successes, or the cumulative probability – the probability of any number of successes up through five. Since we are not interested in the probability of them rolling one seven - or two sevens, or three sevens, and so on up through five –we will put "false." If we had wanted that cumulative probability we would have put "true."

Now consider a case in which a person claims that they can roll four sevens in five rolls. How probable is that? For a start, what they really mean is that they can roll **at least** four sevens in five rolls. We would seem to need the cumulative function of the binomial distribution. However, that would give us the probability of the person rolling four or **fewer** sevens. That isn't what we want.

What we want is the probability of the individual **failing** to roll a seven **one or fewer times.** So what we should do is use the cumulative function on **not** throwing a seven. On the first row of the table we put "1", for we are looking for the probability of one or fewer cases of "not throwing a seven." Line two is still five, while the third line is the probability of **not** throwing a seven: 1-.1667=.8333 (The probability of either throwing a seven or not doing so is 1. The probability of not throwing a seven is one minus the probability of throwing the seven.) On the last line we put "true," for we do want the cumulative probability. Getting 4 or more sevens in five throws would be highly unlikely by chance, having a probability of .003346 This is shown as "formula result" in Box VI-2.

BINOMDIST

Number_s	1	▲	= 1
Trials	5	▲	= 5
Probability_s	.8333	▲	= 0.8333
Cumulative	TRUE	▲	= TRUE

= 0.003346194

Returns the individual term binomial distribution probability.

Probability_s is the probability of success on each trial.

Formula result = 0.003346194   (Cancel)   (OK)

Box VI-2. Failing to throw a seven zero or one times.

Let's check that result a different way. The binomial distribution can tell us the probability of the person throwing exactly five sevens in the five throws, it is 0.000129. It can also tell us the probability of their throwing exactly four sevens, which is 0.003215. The probability that one or the other of these will occur is their sum, .003344. This differs slightly from the number above because of rounding errors. For example we used .8333 above when the actual value would be .8 followed by a string of threes infinitely long.

Those Noisy Parties

Now we can return to the question of the noisy parties. Again we use the cumulative function, and look at things in a way that at first may seem backwards. What we are interested in is the probability of **5 or fewer** of them **not** being on floors one or two – in other words, being on floors 3-20. Framing the question in this way enables us to use the cumulative function of the binomial distribution to find the probability that so few - or even fewer – of the noisy parities should be on upper floors.

BINOMDIST

Number_s	5	▲	=	5
Trials	10	▲	=	10
Probability_s	.9	▲	=	0.9
Cumulative	TRUE	▲	=	TRUE

= 0.001634937

Returns the individual term binomial distribution probability.

Cumulative   is a logical value: for the cumulative distribution function, use
TRUE; for the probability mass function, use FALSE.

Formula result =   0.001634937   (Cancel)   (OK)

Box VI-3. Probability of so few noisy parties Being on upper floors.

That probability is shown in Box VI-3. Five is on the top line, for we are interested in the probability of five or fewer parties being on floors 3-20. There is a ten on the second line representing the number of parties. The number on the third line is the chance probability of a party being on floors 3-20. **It is .9 because they make up 90% of the building.** Finally the last line says "true," for we are interested in a cumulative probability – the probability that **5 or fewer parties** would be in the upper part of the building. We see that the observed distribution of parties is very improbable, occurring less than two times in a thousand by chance. With this function we were able to do a test that we could not do with chi-square because of the low frequencies.

Now let's turn away from statistical tests, useful as they are, and look at one final practical matter in designing your questionnaire.

Making a Multi-item Index

In earlier chapters we have dealt with the situation where you were interested in many different things, and used one item to measure each of them. As we saw, in that case you had ordinal level measurement, and it was appropriate for you to use nonparametric statistics, such as chi-square.

Now we are going to look at the other possibility. Suppose that there are only a couple of things that you are interested in and you want to measure feeling about those things very accurately. If that is the case you will want to make a multiple item scale, called an **index**, to measure attitude towards each of them. Those scales will come close to, or even achieve, interval measurement, and probably will permit you to use parametric statistics based on the normal curve.

Let's make an index and see what we can learn about it.

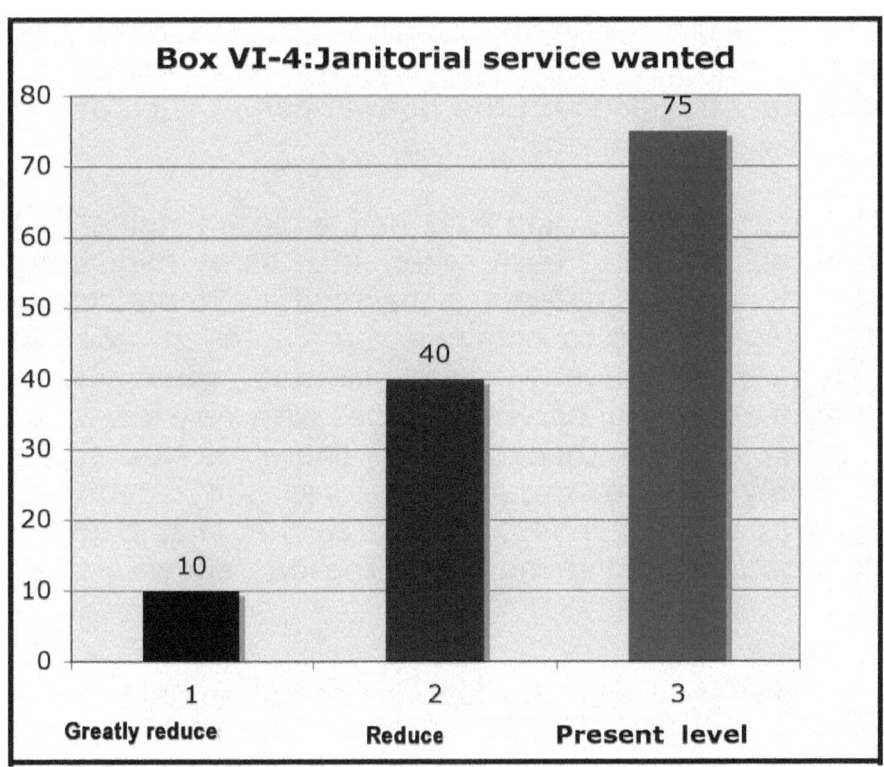

Box VI-4 shows the kind of distribution of scores that you often get on a single item when you survey the members of a condo association. Here we see how many people want how much janitorial service, with the column at the right representing the present level of service. The column at the left shows that ten people favor a drastic reduction in janitorial service. The middle one shows that forty people favor a more moderate cut, while the right hand one shows that seventy-five people favor maintaining the present level of service. Not shown is the number who favor increasing the present level, for that was zero.

The mean score is 2.68. Because the distribution is not symmetrical the mean is not a very good indication of central tendency. In this case the mode, the most common score, would be a better representative of all the scores in the distribution. A symmetrical distribution is also a requirement if you want to run any statistic based on the normal curve, such as the correlation coefficient.

However, suppose you had half a dozen items that were all related to each other, such as by measuring satisfaction with different aspects of life in the condo. You might want to combine them into an index of general satisfaction. That index would probably have a large number of potential values with very few cases making each of those scores. Therefore you would probably want to group the scores into categories, such as 2.0 – 3.9, 4.0 -5.9, etc. That might give a distribution looking more like the one shown in Box VI-5.

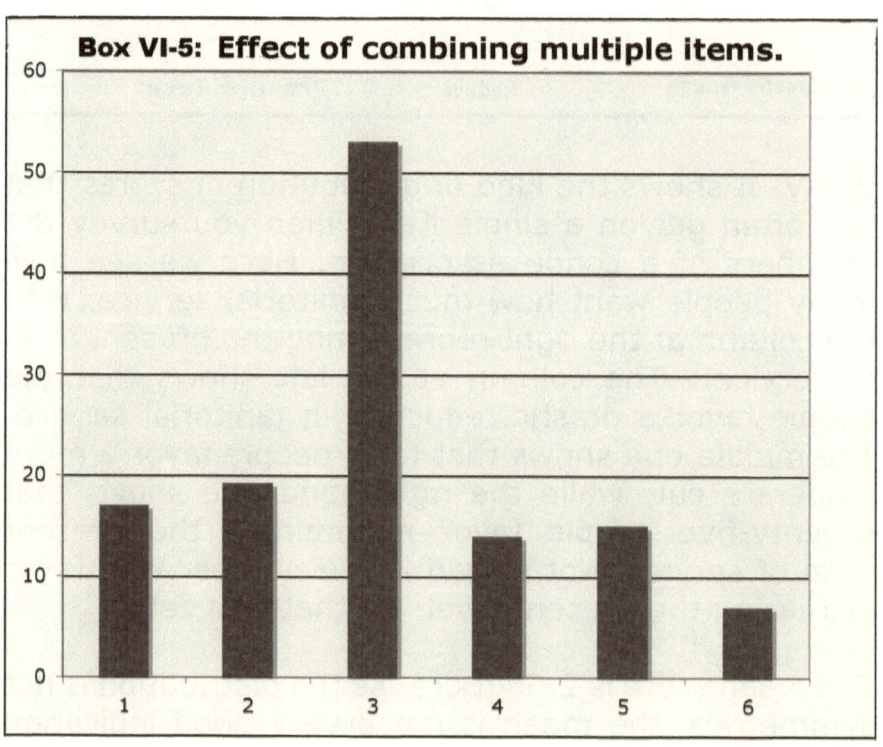

Box VI-5: Effect of combining multiple items.

Let's think a bit more about the scores on our items. Let us assume that the person's **true position** is the score they would get on an interval scale. If we compare the score that one of our items gives to the person with that true position, we see that the situation is just like that portrayed way back in Box II-4. Any given item may over or underestimate the person's favorability to the thing being evaluated. Some items will do one thing and some will do the other.

Looked at this way what we have is measurements with **random error** – that is, error that probably is independent of the person's position on the issue. A lot of items each contributing to the score, and a lot of error terms also making contributions to it, and no factor having a really large effect - why, that is what gives a normal distribution, isn't it?

Without going any further into the reasons, let us note two things that happen as more and more items go into an index: (1) The scores come closer and closer to approximating interval level measurement. (2) Their distribution comes closer and closer to being a normal distribution. **Thus you become more justified in using parametric statistics assuming a normal distribution.**

The situation is analogous to that of giving an exam to students. If you have just one essay item, you may hit on the thing one particular student is best prepared on or the one about which he or she remembers almost nothing. The one item is a very inaccurate measure of that person's knowledge, just as one item on our questionnaire is a very imperfect measure of a respondent's attitude. However, if you use a number of short essay questions, some will overestimate the student's knowledge and some will underestimate it, depending in each case on the overlap between what the item asks about and what the student has studied. Averaging the student's score on a number of items gives a more accurate measure of what the student knows. In the same way, averaging a respondent's score on a number of items gives a more accurate measure of his or her attitude. And, as I mentioned above, as more and more items are averaged it becomes more and more reasonable to use statistics that assume a normal distribution.

Before combining items into an index you will want to make sure that they are positively correlated with each other. If they aren't they aren't measuring the same thing.

Sometimes items are related to each other in surprising ways. A pair of items from my recent survey provides an example. One asked how many hours of concierge duty should be supported. The other asked how many times per day a security firm should patrol the building. One might think that these items would be positively related since they both get at providing security measures. Instead they were very significantly **negatively** correlated!

Comments written by the respondents made clear why that was the case. The most common suggestion for saving money was that the condo association should stop having a concierge on duty at night and instead get frequent patrols by the security firm, a significantly less expensive option. Those people who wanted to cut the hours of the concierge wanted a great number of patrols. On the other hand, many who wanted a concierge 24 hours a day did not see much point in having patrols as well. When you saw how people were thinking the negative correlation made perfect sense.

Summary

So, can we use parametric statistics based on the normal curve on our index scores? There are measures, called *skewness* and *kurtosis* that can be used to see how close a distribution is to a normal one. If the match is good then it is appropriate to use statistics based on the normal distribution. There are also ways of transforming data to get a better fit to a normal distribution. These measures and techniques are beyond what it is appropriate to cover here. As a rough rule of thumb, if your index has a dozen or more items, and the distribution looks reasonably similar to the normal curve, you are probably justified in using normal-curve based statistics. (There are also requirements as to the number of subjects, but surely you will have more than 30 of those.) If your index doesn't meet the requirements for using parametric statistics you can still use them descriptively while testing significance with nonparametric tests. The main thing you will lose is power: effects will have to be stronger to reach statistical significance.

On Your Own

There is a limit to the amount of methodology I can cover without turning this into a statistics text, and unfortunately I have reached it. (Some readers may feel that it was passed long ago.) If you do very much work with indices there are a number of other things that you will want to know. For example:

- How do I test the significance of a correlation coefficient?

•   How do I test the significance of the difference between two means?
•   How do I test whether there is a general effect when a series of means differ?

The first of these questions is fairly easy to answer, at least in technical language. If "n" is the number of cases that the coefficient is based upon and "r" is the correlation coefficient, then

$$\frac{(n-2)\ r^2}{1-r^2}$$

may be tested in a variance ratio table with 1 and n-2 degrees of freedom.

The second question would require a lengthier answer, and the third would lead into the depths of analysis of variance. For an explanation of these, and other matters that go beyond what I have covered, you are referred to any standard statistics text. Similarly, there are more specialized attitude measurement texts that cover the multi-item scaling techniques that I have not included. Despite the existence of those more sophisticated techniques, you can go a long way with the simpler tools that we have covered.

In Conclusion

The Final Report

To the Board. The main purpose of your survey is to inform the Board, so we will first look at your report to them. You should consider 1) how inclusive it should be, and 2) the handling of potentially confidential materials.

Inclusiveness. One question is the amount of discussion of methodology to include in the report. In scientific research publications one includes a detailed enough description of how the study was done so that someone else could follow the same procedures and presumably get the same result. You should be able to include this if the Board wants it. They may want it in a separate document, or not at all.

Even if they do want it, remember that it does not mean that you have to include every detail of what you did. The test is whether the information is an essential part of the procedures. For example, if you did guarantee anonymity, it may be enough to say that you followed the Oregon System – if that is what you did – without telling who did what when and how to achieve that. If you did a follow-up of nonrespondents two weeks after first distribution of the questionnaires, it is enough to say that without giving, for example, the date of each contact. Give only essential details.

Results that are not statistically significant. A second area where decisions must be made about what to include has to do with nonsignificant results. One position is that nothing should be reported unless it is significant. Warning Board members that they should disregard some result because it is very likely simply a matter of chance may be like telling jury members to disregard some testimony that they have heard. It is easier said than done.

Another position is that the matter should be approached in terms of cost benefit analysis. Are the consequences of the Board believing this if is not true more or less severe than the consequences of them not believing it if it is true? Although of only marginal significance I included in the report to my Board that both communication by them and how they dealt with complaints were rated lower than any of the other things being evaluated in that section of the questionnaire. I thought that the consequences of them not knowing this if it was a reliable finding were potentially worse than those resulting from them believing it if it was just chance operating in our sample. In any case, if nonsignificant results are included it should be made clear that that is what they are.

Individual or only group results? To what extent should individual comments be summarized, or even included in full, in the report?

There are probably too many to include all of them. If that is not done, what can be?

If you did not use content analysis to refine your questions after the pretest, this may be the time to use it now. First you should probably not feel too bad about discarding comments that exactly mirror the fixed response already given. If you ask, "How important is it to you to have fresh flowers in the lobby?" and the respondent checks "very important," then you may not need to code it when he writes as a comment, "It is very important to me to have fresh flowers in the lobby."

Beyond that you are bound to find that most responses fall in a few fairly predictable categories and can simply be counted. This again, however, is a point where judgment is required. Even if only given by one person, an insightful observation or unique suggestion should be included in your summary. If only one person notes that the garage walls are leaking it should still be reported.

Privacy. Even with anonymous questionnaires questions of privacy may arise as a result of individual comments on questionnaires. If someone prefaces their remarks by saying, "I own two large dogs" or "I have several times complained about noise on my floor" then any reader is likely to know who that person is. If they then make a suggestion that they have made before, and it is not made by others, then it would be best not to quote them. If a number of other people make the same comment or suggestion, then the identifiable person's comment may be included in the category.

Because there no names associated with the identifying numbers on the questionnaires the entire database can be given to the Board on disk if they want it. Members who are methodologically sophisticated may want to do additional analyses.

To Others. I hope that your arrangements with the Board are such that you can distribute a report to the entire membership of the Condominium Association. As mentioned earlier this is their only reward for helping you with your research.

It is more than that, however. Where a person lives is often a very important part of his or her self-conception, as well as an indication of relative status to others. The report is in some ways an advertising brochure, even if its recipients are already owners and residents. You should do all that you can to make them feel good about themselves and where they live. That does not mean that you should distort the study's findings. It does mean that, to the extent that your resources permit, you should make your report look like an advertisement for a Mercedes of BMW. Maybe you still want to distribute it by hand so that you can point out how much you have saved on postage, but in other ways this is where you want to be lavish rather than frugal.

A report to the general membership does not need to be very long, but it should be in full color. The main findings can be presented in full color three-dimensional graphs. There should be no discussion of methodology and no summary of comments. Instead it should just hit the high points, leaving the details for the Board. It should come out as soon as possible after the study is completed.

Postscript

You now know what I can teach you about how to study your condo association. From this point on it is just a matter of using common sense in applying what you know.

I have tried in this book to give you general principles that will enable you to work out the details for yourself. Some areas have been covered more thoroughly than others. I have barely touched on sampling - a specialized field in itself - for I have assumed that your association is probably small enough that you will try to include everyone. As already mentioned, I have passed over formal scaling techniques as being more elaborate than suit your purposes.

There is one way in which the study I did failed to live up to the principles given here, and it should serve as a caution to you. I did not do as thorough a pretest as I advocate in this book. I let the Board pressure me into skimping there in order to save time. The result was that some questions were not formulated as well as they should have been, leading the respondents to write more comments than they would have otherwise. Content analyzing those comments was a major contribution of one of my coworkers. Time was wasted, not saved, in the end.

It is difficult – sometimes impossible – to do the study just as it should be done. That is one of the prices of working in the real world.

Good luck in your undertaking.

Index

A

Acuña, Rodolfo 17
Anonymity 7, 17, 20, 99
Association, Condo 7, 8, 23, 29, 41, 93, 96, 102
Avoiding Errors 49

B

Backups 51
Binomdist 88
Binomial expansion 81, 86
Board, Condo 5, 15, 20, 21, 22, 99, 100, 101, 102, 103

C

Chi-square test 27
Clever Hans 13
Coding 5, 27, 43, 44, 47, 48, 49, 50, 51, 55, 66
Coding sheet 27, 47, 48, 49, 50, 51, 66
Content analysis 100
Context 7, 17, 18, 19, 39
Correlation 27, 36, 37, 74, 94, 97, 98
Correlation coefficient 36, 37, 94, 97, 98
Cost 13, 17, 18, 20, 21, 46, 100
Count if 67
Cumulative 88, 89, 90, 91

D

Data 26, 37, 38, 39, 42, 43, 44, 45, 46, 47, 48, 49, 50, 51, 52, 54, 60, 61, 63, 64, 66, 67, 69, 70, 71, 72, 78, 79, 80, 81, 83, 84, 97
Databank 47, 48, 51, 66
Datasheet 47, 51, 66, 67

E

Error, random 95
Errors, avoiding 49
Errors, coding 51
Errors, programming 50
Ethics 14, 15, 19, 20
Ethnic identity 24
Exercises 69
Expected frequencies 71

O

Observed Frequencies 71
Ordinal 27, 36, 37, 71, 84, 92
Oregon system 99
Owners, nonresident 22
Owners of multiple units 9

P

Parameters 61, 62
Parametric statistics 37, 92, 95, 97
Parkinson, C. Northcote 45, 46
Parties, noisy 71, 72, 80, 81, 82, 90
Paste special 51, 64, 67
Pfungst, Oskar 14
Pretest 14, 38, 39, 41, 42, 43, 44, 46, 49, 52, 100, 103
Privacy 22, 101
Probability, two laws of 85
Push Polling 11

Q

Questions 4, 7, 11, 12, 13, 18, 21, 26, 27, 38, 39, 40, 41, 42, 43, 44, 45, 46, 52, 53, 95, 98, 100, 101, 103
Questions, open-ended 26, 38, 42, 52, 53

R

Ratio 27, 31, 32, 37, 98
Redundancy 50, 51
Respondents, motivating 19, 101. *See also* Trust
Results, nonsignificant 99, 100

S

"Success" in binomial distribution 86, 87, 88, 89, 90
Sampling 5, 7, 8, 45, 102
Scatter plot 73, 74
Self-conception 24, 26, 102
Self-presentation 37
Significance, statistical 29, 30, 97
Skewness 97
Spreadsheet 30, 47, 53, 54, 55, 60, 63, 64, 65, 66, 67, 70, 76, 77, 78, 88
Stubbornness 3
Sum, Σ 55, 61
Sum if 67, 68, 69, 70

T

Trust 4, 5, 15, 19, 20, 23, 24

Y

Yates' correction 80